The Nearness of God

Breige O'Hare

The Nearness of God

© Breige O'Hare 2011

ISBN 978-0-9566885-7-6

Categories: Catholic Faith, Theology, Spiritual growth, Prayer

Published in 2011 by Shanway Press, Belfast. Contact info@shanway.com

CONTENTS   PAGE

Introduction   5

1. From the Beginning: The Nearness of God   16
in Creation

2. Led by Love: The Nearness of God in his   30
Word

3. Love is Strong as Death: Jesus as the   52
Nearness of God

4. Becoming What You Receive: The   74
Nearness of God in the Body of Christ

5. Come! Baptism as Christ's invitation to   98
Nearness

6. Where Are You? The Nearness of You   120

7. Knowing What Matters: Resting in the   138
Nearness of God.

Suggestions for Further Reading   157

Chapter Notes   158

Do you remember the last time you felt thirsty, when every part of you ached with dry-mouthed longing for the relief that only a slow, cool drink could bring? Thankfully, the experience is rare enough; these temperate isles of ours are lands of lush green meadows; we are well catered for in our turn-on-the-tap houses. Warm summer showers follow fast on the heels of cold, unrelenting winter rains. If drought comes, it comes as a tourist: foreign, fleeting, its impact short-lived.

Our world is full of water, yet still we thirst; we are born wanting . . . wanting . . . something. We spend lives longing to satisfy some felt lack within us, some primal ache that we cannot fully identify and do not really understand; looking in the places of power and possession; seeking out the fleeting sugar-rushes provided by new clothes, new lovers, new gadgets.

Yet these things just will not do; our deepest thirsts will not be sated by such things. Even our most elaborate and extravagant attempts to indulge our desires bring only temporary relief from the ache which fills us to the depths of our being. We are not born wanting something; we are born wanting God. The thirst that both torments and thrills us is our thirst for God: nothing else will satisfy.

This book addresses our thirst for God by offering a chance to explore the ordinary places in our lives and to rediscover there the only One who will satisfy the deepest desires and longings of our hearts. It sets out to help

INTRODUCTION

A WORLD FULL OF GOD

God's
imperishable
spirit
is in all things
Wisdom 11:26;12:1

us to revisit these ordinary places and, perhaps, to experience them differently, deeply. In using the book as a guide, we hope to stumble upon God amid the ups-and-downs of daily life and there to be reminded and reassured that God is with us in every movement, every breath, every drop of our existence.

In these opening pages of our journey, we start in what may seem to be a place of strange beginnings for those of us intent upon slaking thirst. We begin our quest in the desert, that place of drought where thirst is a constant companion to the unforgiving intensity of the sun's rays; a dusty wilderness; a land without water, without life, without prospect or promise. The desert has much to teach us about slaking our God-thirst. However, its lessons are not the obvious ones, as you will discover.

New life

We often imagine deserts in terms of vast tracts of undulating sand dunes or dry and rocky expanses and so we might be forgiven for entertaining the notion that little or no life survives in the desert. We would be wrong. Certain creatures have made a home of what seems to be empty and dead terrain, evolving many different strategies in their attempts to outdo the blistering sun. Some plants, dealt a lucky hand of genes, survive in crevices or beneath sand surface; leaves dried up, life processes slowed down so that their need for water is greatly reduced.

They sit in precarious shelter, a dried up version of themselves, poised and ready for the coming of rare and precious desert rains. When rain does come, its impact seems nothing short of miraculous. In a matter of minutes, plants' shrivelled leaves swell and unfurl. Soon, blossoms open and seedpods develop. The desert changes, the once dead landscape now dotted with patches of greenest green. New growth emerges; a life of unfolding and unfurling exposed; a fuller and a fruitful life.

Even if we know little about plants or deserts, we can picture the almost magical scene that unfolds in response to the coming of the desert rains. These apparently dead plants seem to have been brought back to life, their leaves regenerated from dusty skeletal remains. The air of mystery is dispelled by botanical fact: these sad-looking specimens were not dead but merely desiccated. Nevertheless, their common name endures, giving some sense of their apparently miraculous restoration; they are called 'resurrection plants'.

 ## Living water . . . God's offer of new life

The ingenious resurrection plants furnish us not only with examples of the transforming impact of water upon a parched landscape, but also with an image to help us understand an infinitely more mysterious transformation – that of the transformation wrought by the profound impact of God's presence on our humanity. The desert plant awaits the life-giving rains. Our humanity opens itself instead to attentions of another kind: the life-giving Living Water of the Holy Spirit.

Of course, the Living Water on offer from God is not something separate from God, but God's gift of himself, Father Son and Spirit. In this way, God is not only offering life to us, he is offering us *his* life. Contained within that offer is the promise of new life; a share in God's own life, in God's eternal life.

. . . no one who drinks the water that I shall give will ever be thirsty again The water that I shall give will become a spring of water within, welling up for eternal life.
John 4: 14

Desert rains transform the life of the resurrection plant into something lush and fruitful, the presence of water within its leaves causing them to extend out beyond the dark crevices where the plant has until now sheltered, unseen. God's Living Water - God's gift of himself - wells up deep within each one of us, offering us eternal life, the chance to extend out beyond the shrivelled margins of a self-centred existence. The offer is of a fuller and more fruitful life; a life centred on God; a life lived in love with God, Father, Son and Spirit.

Thirsting for God

From shrivelled self to full and fruitful life: the resurrection plant's story may provide an image to help us to move a little way in our understanding of God's transforming presence within our humanity but it fails miserably to convey the totality of God's availability to us and the generosity of his presence within us. With God, there is no drought, no waiting for water. As we shall be reminded in the pages below, God's Living Water, the Holy Spirit, is in all things, permeating and animating every aspect of our existence; always and in all ways. We live in a *world of wet*,[1] a world full of God.[2]

Lord your imperishable spirit is in everything.
Wisdom 11:26; 12:1

The word of God and his Breath are at the origin of the being and life of every creature
CCC #703

God, you are my God, I pine for you. my heart thirsts for you my body longs for you, as a land parched, dreary and waterless.
Psalm 63:1

I thirst for God, the living God; when shall I go to see the face of God?
Psalm 42:2

A world of wet: these words of the priest-poet, Gerard Manley Hopkins, articulate not his joy at the experience of a world full of God but his struggle in finding some sense of relief from his God-thirst. Such thirst, he suggests, will not be quenched, even in this world of wet. Hopkins captures something of our human condition: God is with us . . . yet still we thirst for him.

Hopkins also captures sentiments expressed thousands of years ago by the psalmists. Their pleas are familiar to us; sitting in the dust of our frustrated longing, we feel in their words the aching dryness of our own desires.

Like the psalmists, we, too, can find ourselves asking where we might go to know God's presence, to be reassured that he is with us even in what seems like parched and weary desert land. How can we satisfy this thirst for Living Water? Where can we see the face of God?

When you search for me,
you will find me;
when you search
wholeheartedly for me,
I shall let you find me
Jeremiah 29:13

As we try to reason with and struggle with our thirst, we might remind ourselves that God's infinite and mysterious presence is elusive. This is true; we are in relationship with a God who evades our most strenuous efforts to understand or contain him. God will always be more, more than our intellect and senses can comprehend. We will find ourselves constantly engaged in that search for more; always looking, always thirsting. The argument is accurate, convincing. However, at some level also, deep down, we suspect that some of the "more" of God could be within our reach . . . if only we knew where to look.

. . . concerning God, we
cannot grasp what he is.
CCC #43
(quoting Thomas Aquinas)

This book is a journey in search of the more of God, focussing our search amid the ordinary nuts-and -bolts of daily life. It is a search for a God who wants to be known by us. The God we seek wants to be found. Yet from the outset, we know that our journey will have its frustrations. We are engaging with Mystery; God will always evade our clever attempts at capture and part of our journey will involve our living with the tension of our unanswered questions about God, recognising . . . again . . . that in this quest for God we are not alone: he is with us.

The Nearness of God

God wants to be with us, to give himself to us. Karl Rahner, one of the theologians who made a major contribution to Vatican II, puts it beautifully:[3]

> For what does Christianity really declare? Nothing else, after all, than that the great Mystery remains eternally a mystery, but that this mystery wishes to communicate Himself in absolute self-communication – as the infinite, incomprehensible and inexpressible Being whose name is God, as self-giving nearness –to the human soul in the midst of its experience of its own finite emptiness.

. . . this mystery wishes to communicate Himself . . . as self-giving nearness . . . Rahner's words help to provide the focus for our journey through this book. Rahner writes in German but the word 'nearness' is used to translate his sense of God's availability. It is more than the proximity of one person near 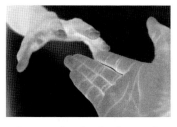 to another in a room; it points to the experience of a God who makes himself available to us in self-gift: God is near to us because God gives us God. We are setting off together to explore and experience for ourselves the nearness of a God who has given, is giving, himself to each one of us.

The focus has been expressed in this way to carry Rahner's sense of the self-giving availability of God, but we also hear the word nearness as it is used in the sense in which it appears in the old Carmichael and Washington classic, 'The Nearness of You'. There, it conveys a lover's thrill at being with the one he loves. "It's not the pale moon that excites me; that thrills and delights me. Oh no, it's just the nearness of you," the love-struck songster declares. For him, the experience of nearness to her is electrifying, breath-taking, all-consuming.

As we proceed, we will grow to appreciate that the lover's thrill is a mutual dimension of the experience of the nearness of God. God is excited to be with us; we are in love with a God who is passionately in love with us. However, we may also experience the nearness of God in a different way: nearness is never near enough. The God of intimate nearness is the God of infinite distance; our thirst will always remain unquenched in this world of wet.

> *Whether we realise it or not, prayer is the encounter of God's thirst with ours.*
> *God thirsts that we may thirst for him.*
> CCC #2560

Strangely enough, however painful the experience of our God-thirst may be, we might regard it as one of God's many gifts to us and even appreciate it as a necessary part of our journey. It has been planted within us by a God who thirsts for us first. If we pay attention to thirst's leading, it will keep us going in the right direction; our thirst will be our homing device; it will keep us wanting God, help us to find our home in him. Thirst will sharpen and intensify our longing; it will help us find what our hearts desire and to discover the truth again - that only Living Water will bring us the relief we seek. Our hearts will not rest until they rest in God. [4] Nothing else but God will do.

 Our journey ahead

God is so very near to us - if only we knew where to look. The sad fact is that, as a Church, we once knew where to look; Paul's letters are full of indications of the experience of the Risen Jesus and of the Spirit's presence and action in the daily lives and in the liturgies of those early communities. However, over the centuries, we have tended to redirect our attentions and to focus in those places and people we thought of as particularly 'holy'. In doing so, we overlooked the God who lives in all things, the Living Water who creates for us this world of wet, who shares with us a world full of God.

We already know that we live in a world full of God. Therefore, our task is not so much about 'finding' God as changing the lenses through which we view our world so that we might bring the God who is already near to us into sharper focus. In this book, we aim to refocus together and to become more aware of God's transforming presence at work amid the nuts and bolts of what may seem to us at times to be a very ordinary and mundane existence.

Over the course of the following chapters, we hope to see again the self-giving nearness of God in our creation and in God's Word. We will reflect on Jesus as the ultimate self-giving nearness of God and explore the experience of the nearness of God, as sustained by the presence and action of God's Holy Spirit in Christ's Body, the Church.

We will look at the ways in which that Spirit remains present to us in our daily lives and in our liturgies, reflecting also on the ways in which God's nearness is made visible and touchable through the sacraments of our Church and their impact on us. The final two chapters will be an invitation to reflect in a very personal way on our own unique experience of God's nearness to us and to explore and accept our experiences of felt-distance from God.

This book is a presentation of relevant teaching from a variety of sources, and endnotes are provided for those who wish to consult those sources. However, mindful that the word 'water' never quenched a thirst, the book is primarily designed as an invitation to experience. Needless to say, we cannot engineer an experience of the nearness of God; God's touch is subtle; he has his own way of being with each one of us. Both reader and writer are simply invited to trust that God has matters in hand and that the primary task on this journey together is to "Let God be God."[5]

While we cannot contrive experiences of God, we can at least open ourselves to possibilities. To this end, each chapter closes with suggestions for prayer and reflection to help us to engage with the material in the context of our own experience of relationship with God. It would be good not to skip over the prayer and reflection suggestions. Not all will suit. However, they are an important part of the journey. They will help to achieve the aim of this book, which is to create a companionable space within which to experience something of God's nearness and, in that experience, to enable God to do what God will do.

Finally, we embark upon our shared mission remembering that, however much we are searching and thirsting for God and for that elusive 'more', God has taken the initiative and is already searching and thirsting for us. He thirsts that we might thirst for him; he searches that we might search too. Do not worry; we are already found; he is here with us now. We will take our time going through this book, trusting ourselves to be in his presence. Settle into it and discover the pieces that help each one of us to find our own unique way to grow in awareness of the nearness of God in our own life. Be prepared to be surprised.

Velle Deum esse Deum

. . . Let God be God.

FOR YOUR PRAYER AND REFLECTION

God is with us at all times and you have your own way of attending to his presence. Throughout this book, in particular at the end of each chapter, you will find suggestions to support and affirm your ongoing way of relating to God during those specific times we refer to as prayer. The express purpose of focussing on these specific times is to help you to relate to the God who is communicating with you at all times.

The suggestions made will always be simple; as with close friendships, relationships are deepened by apparently small gestures because they are imbued with great significance, because they are gestures of love.

SUGGESTION ONE: Growing in awareness of God with you.

The gentle repetition of a verse of scripture can be a reassuring way of staying in touch with God's presence in your day, however near or far-away God may seem to you. Repetition can lead to insight, instil calm, or provide a welcome anchor amid the choppy seas of life. Repeat the words throughout your day. Let them be your words to God. Let them lead you into the conversation you need to have with him. A few examples:

When you search for me, you will find me; when you search wholeheartedly for me, I will let you find me. Jeremiah 29:13

God, you are my God, I pine for you; my heart thirsts for you, my body longs for you as a land parched, dreary and waterless. Psalm 63:1

14

SUGGESTION TWO: On a journey together.

Repeat the Latin words slowly and gently.

Velle Deum esse Deum

Let God be God.

Let the rhythm of the Latin (Veh-lay day-um ess-say day-um) lull you into restfulness and help you to slow down. Use the connection that Latin provides with history to remind you that you seek and find God in the company of others who have gone before you and shared the journey. You are not alone

How can this be? (Luke 1:34) Mary's words to the angel Gabriel, words of wonder and awe, found an echo in my own heart when I sensed the first flutter of my baby's gentle movement within my womb. I struggled to give expression to the amazement I felt at this new life, with its own personality, its own destiny, growing and moving inside me; God was creating her in me, bringing her to life in me.

Holding this tiny creature in my arms a few moments after her birth was an experience beyond my wildest imaginings. Heart pounding with excitement and delight, I gazed at her and knew with every fibre of my being that I would do anything to care for and protect her. I would give my life for this wonderful, wonderful child: she belonged to me and I belonged to her.

As we set off on the journey of this book, we do so in the hope that we might grow in awareness of the nearness of God. The experience of mother-love is a good place to start because it is in this bond of love between mother and child that we are presented with something of the love and longing of the creator God.

Such is the mother-father God, the source of life; the God who has loved us into life and who wants to be with us to share the life and love he has given us. Such is the God who whispers into the tiny ear of each baby he has created, 'I am yours and you are mine'.[1] God wants nearness with us. His entire creation is focussed on bringing about that nearness and

1. FROM THE BEGINNING

THE NEARNESS OF GOD IN CREATION

I belong to my love and my love belongs to me.
Song of Songs 6:3

has been from the beginning. We are created for absolute nearness with God; we belong with him; nothing less will do.

This chapter presents an opportunity to reflect upon and to pray with a deepening awareness of God's nearness to us in creation. It begins with a disclaimer: no words will ever capture the mystery of the divine love that called creation into being and gave it life. No expression will convey the vastness of the love and longing that gave birth to our humanity with one generous purpose in mind: *so that Love could bestow itself on us*.[2] Nothing will capture the depth of desire of a God who set creation in motion so that he could give himself to us.

In spite of our improved scientific knowledge and access to beautiful and skilfully crafted images of God's creation, we must begin our journey with the awareness that even our finest efforts will only serve to scratch the surface of this universe of evolving complexity, a universe set in motion by God. Our human eyes will catch merely a glimpse of the God who is so profoundly and purposefully present to us in a creation that reflects the beauty and balance of the creator.[3]

 ## God's Spirit

With our disclaimer firmly in place, we can admire the skill of the writers of Genesis[4] who were grappling with the profound and unfathomable mystery of God's presence and purpose in creation. Writing without the benefit of Christian insight and scientific knowledge,[5] they used the powerful imagery and symbolism of their time to weave together a story of our human beginnings in a relationship of absolute nearness with God. Although not to be taken literally - the texts *present the work of the creator symbolically*[6] - their story highlights profound truths about God and his nearness to us in creation. Genesis provides us with a useful place from which to embark upon our search for the nearness of God – we return to the Genesis account of the beginning of creation.

The curtain rises on the story of creation, with Genesis' writers placing God centre-stage using imagery that is often overlooked by our 21st century eyes. God is mentioned explicitly but his nearness is also represented in symbolic form: God is the wind sweeping over the waters. The Hebrew word used in the text to render 'wind' is *ruach*,[7] a feminine noun. *Ruach* is breath: God's life-giving breath. *Ruach* is spirit: God's Spirit. *Ruach* offers the reader a Hebrew word-picture of a God intimately involved in his creation from the beginning.

In the beginning, God created
heaven and the earth.
Now the earth was a formless void,
there was darkness over the deep,
with a divine wind sweeping over the waters.
Genesis 1: 1-2

The image of the Spirit sweeping over the waters has additional significance if we understand that water is an ancient symbol of chaos.[8] Used in this way in the Genesis text, the image points to the purposeful nearness of God. God is operating within the chaos to bring about order. The nearness of God is bearing fruit in a world of beauty and diversity, of harmony and balance; everything in its right place; reflecting the beauty and the diversity that exists in the loving union of the Trinity.[9] In Genesis, we have the story of a creation filled with God and centred on God, subject to his will, sharing his love, fulfilling his dreams. *'You are mine and I am yours,'* the creator God whispers, heart pounding with excitement and delight at the promise of self-giving, life-giving relationship with his beloved creatures.

This story of the intimate involvement of the creator God and his Spirit-Breath in creation communicates a conviction that was deeply held by the original Hebrew readers of the text: that *without the Creator, the creature vanishes.*[10] The Spirit-breath permeates and sustains all of life; Genesis invites us to recognise the self-giving nearness of God as an intrinsic and essential part of our creation. It is God sharing his life with God's creation. God's life is no added extra: without God's life-giving presence, creation cannot exist.

 Alive with the breath of God

Having assembled for us this original cast of creatures and in a fashion typical of writers of their time, the authors of Genesis choose one character, Adam - the word means "man" - as a symbol of humanity.[11] Unlike the other creatures, Adam is created in God's *image and likeness* (Genesis 1:26). Loved into being, sustained by that love, Adam's purpose is to share in the self-giving union of the Trinity;

For man would not exist were he not created by God's love and constantly preserved by it
Vatican II
Gaudium et Spes #19

Adam's destiny is to be united with God's life, to live in God's love.[12]

The Genesis account continues with God breathing his Holy breath into Adam. With this, Adam becomes a man *'alive with the breath of God'*.[13]

19

Then Yahweh God formed Man,
dust drawn from the clay,
and breathed into his nostrils a breath of life
and Man became alive with breath.
Genesis 2:7

Adam is *alive!* He is alive with God's breath, alive with God's Spirit! Genesis thus furnishes us with a word-picture of the Spirit living within our Adam-humanity, a dynamic energizing experience of the self-giving nearness of God. The Genesis story captures the beginning of God's life-giving nearness to us. It was a beginning that would eventually come to its fullest and final form in Jesus; the One fully alive with the breath of God.[14] Jesus would be humanity's destination. In Adam, we get some sense of humanity's start and it is a good start. In Adam, we see the opening act of God's plan for relationship with our humanity; God loving Adam into life; Adam living in love with God.

> *God is love.*
> *Whoever*
> *lives in love*
> *lives in God,*
> *and God in them.*
> 1 John 4: 16b

At this point it would be good to remember that being loved by God is more than simply receiving love from God, as if such love were a gift parcelled up and given from the outside. To be loved by God is to be invited *into* God's love. More than this, to be loved by God is to share in God's *way* of loving.[15] Therefore, when the writers of Genesis place the woman Eve on the set of the Genesis story, they create a couple whose love for each other is a sharing in the love of Father, Son and Spirit and a sharing in the qualities of that love: mutual generosity, loving concern and selfless attention to each other.[16]

Living-in-Love; in Genesis, we have Adam and Eve existing in harmonious relationship with God and with each other. Little wonder that when the writers of Genesis choose a set for their story it is a garden of greenest green: Eden. With Eden, we have the writers' image of what the world would be like, if lived in absolute self-giving nearness with God: a lush and fertile paradise; a world full of God; humanity alive with the breath of God; centred on God's dream; fulfilling God's purpose: a full and fruitful life.

What happened?

God created a paradise of love for his beloved humanity. Where is it now? The Eden paradise of Genesis is definitely not the setting in which we find ourselves today nor does it resemble the stage upon which our humanity has played its savage and selfish dramas over many centuries. Designed for a relationship of self-giving nearness, created to live in the paradise of God's love; yet here we sit in our 21st century seats reading a book to help us rediscover the nearness of God in our world. We have been created to be alive with the breath of God, to live fully in this world of wet, this world full of God. What happened?

The writers of Genesis did not have the answer to the "What happened?" question. They knew only that, over the period of their writing Genesis, a worrying number of the people of Israel had lost faith in the nearness of the God of the covenant and were opting instead for Eastern fertility cults.[17] These cults we see depicted in the Genesis account under the guise of one of the fertility symbols they adopted as their own: the serpent. The serpent slinks in and out of the shadows, its appearance unpleasant, its actions often deadly. In Genesis, it serves as a skilfully chosen metaphor for writers wishing not only to identify the target of their scorn but also to emphasise the subtle nature of the evil to which their own people were being exposed.[18]

As the Genesis story unfolds, Adam and Eve follow the same script as the people of Israel at the time that this section of Genesis was written. The story points to the past and to the Hebrew readers' present, to past choices and to choices being made by the readers' contemporaries. God had given humanity free choice so that men and women might choose to live in love with God, and to live in ways that please him.[19] Adam and Eve bring into full focus a humanity that exercises its freedom in ways that are damaging and that do not please the loving creator God who wants only good for

> *God willed that man should be 'left in the hand of his own counsel,' so that he might of his own accord seek his Creator . . .* CCC #1750

his beloved creation. The Genesis story presents the couple eating fruit from the forbidden Tree of Knowledge. Here is humanity doing what it wants, rather than what God wants.

Eating the fruit from the Tree of Knowledge brings Adam and Eve a new awareness of themselves and we can almost imagine them blushing at what they perceive to be their nakedness. The irony of their situation is not lost on us. After eating the fruit of the Tree of Knowledge, Adam and Eve think that they are able to see themselves more clearly. In reality, they have never been so blind. In their act of wilful disobedience, they lose sight of their identity as creatures and their total dependence on their loving creator.

 ME-first

Self-seeking, self-absorbed, mistrusting, misled; Adam and Eve are images of our sad and selfish humanity. They depict a humanity that has fallen short of what God has created it to be. Adam and Eve stand as representatives of a humanity that has weakened the bond with God, rupturing the relationship of loving trust, destroying the blissful paradise of a life that was the fruit of sustained openness to God's self-giving nearness.

Adam and Eve make choices that shift their focus from God to their own selfish selves. They act as if they are creators of their own lives and forget their total dependence on God. In spite of the fact that they inhabit a world alive with the nearness of God, they choose something other than God as a means of satisfying their fickle and fleeting desires.

We have a word for this kind of attitude and activity; we call it SIN. We so often reduce sin to an item on a list and in doing so we have diminished its meaning. The Genesis story highlights sin as a stance in relation to God, a way of viewing life that puts ME-first rather than GOD-first. Such a stance rarely results in a total rejection of God, but instead influences a thousand apparently small decisions, each decision disrupting the delicate balance of a creation designed for harmony, a creation with God at its centre.[20]

The impact of sin on our humanity is emphasised in Genesis by the couple's altered attitude towards God. No longer do Adam and Eve trust in God's loving generosity; no longer do they heed God's wisdom nor respect God's will for them. Step by small step, they move away from God - towards the tree, away with the fruit - to hide in the bushes. ME-first: the effects of sin leak like acid into their lives, corroding relationships with God and with each other, damaging the harmony and balance within the wonderful existence that God has created for them.

Sin - disobedience toward God and lack of trust in his goodness.
CCC #397

. . . refusing to acknowledge God as his source, man has also upset the relationship which should link him to his last end
CCC #401

God is pure goodness and what God creates can only be good.[21] However, the Genesis account is a stark reminder that sin seems to have been part of our make-up from our earliest times.[22] A reading of our history is all that is necessary to confirm this. Littered with the debris of wars, famine and persecution, our records of relationships with each other bear witness to our need to satisfy our own ME-first desires for power and wealth and comfort.

Although conflict may only directly stem from and affect a limited number of people at any particular time in our history, we live within intricate webs of interconnecting relationships and we suffer from inner

conflict as a result. The virus of sin has a way of infecting us all; we live as divided selves, unable to open ourselves fully to God's offer of nearness, born needing help to overcome the assaults of evil. Benedict XVI, writing before he was elected Pope, reminds us that every human being enters a world that is . . .

. . . *marked by relational damage. At the very moment a person begins human existence which is good, he or she is confronted by a sin-damaged world. Each of us enters into a situation in which relationship has been hurt. Consequently, each person is, from the start, damaged in relationships and does not engage in them as he or she ought. Sin pursues the human being and he or she capitulates to it.*[23]

 Faithful God

Humanity continues to suffer from the effects of its ME-first small-minded self-absorption. Yet the very tale of our original downfall, our succumbing to the desires of our selfish selves, is also presented by the authors of Genesis as a tale of enduring hope. They do not abandon themselves or their readers to a spiral of despair but show instead that, in spite of Adam and Eve's NO to God's dream for them, God never says NO to his dream for his beloved creation.

> *God loves this child . . . from eternity . . .There was never a moment . . . that this life, this person and his eternal destiny were not . . . embraced in His Divine love.*
> Karl Rahner

As already noted above, scripture reveals a God who remains present within his creation as the source of its life. God's self-giving nearness endures; God remains present within Adam, within our humanity.[24] He continues to give life to his creatures. Each person created is sustained by contact with God's divine energy; each child, an unrepeatable[25] reflection, a unique and irreplaceable image, of the unfathomable mystery of the Creator-God. Each child loved from the beginning; each loved into being.[26]

Our flawed and fickle couple, Adam and Eve, provide us with a literary image of humanity on the cusp of God's vast plan for his creation. Thousands of years after the writing of Genesis, the apostle Paul elaborates further on what he understands as God's plan for his beloved humanity, a plan beginning with creation and brought to fruition through Christ. Christ would restore humanity so that we could live again united in self-giving nearness with God. Paul's words are caught again in the writings of the second century bishop Tertullian.[27]

> *In all the form which was moulded in the clay, Christ was in his [God's] thoughts as the human being who was to be.*
> Tertullian 2nd Century Bishop of Carthage

25

We are running ahead of ourselves. At this early stage of our journey, we need only remember and be reassured by our knowledge that the Genesis story is not a tale of ending. God does not abandon humanity to its small and shrivelled ME-first world. Instead, we see a God who pledges himself relentlessly to fostering a relationship of self-giving nearness with Adam and with his descendants.[28]

At this point, we take our leave of Adam who has put himself centre-stage, miscasting himself in the leading role in the unfolding drama of creation. We can be grateful that, for God, our human story was not a divine and elaborate drama but a relentless quest to bring his creation home to live in love with him. God did not waver in his task, and in the chapter that follows, we will see how God's offer of self-giving nearness to his people continued. In their story, we hope to recognise our own. We hope to hear, again and again, the God who proclaims his devotion to his beloved children. '*I belong to you and you belong to me,*' God whispers into their hearts. '*I am yours and you are mine*'.

FOR YOUR PRAYER AND REFLECTION

SUGGESTION ONE: Alive with the breath of God

Use your breath to help you to come to an awareness of the Spirit-Breath within you, to remind you of God's gift of life. There is no need to change the pattern or rhythm of your breathing; simply notice your breathing as you breathe in and out. You have God's life within you, whether you are consciously aware of that life or not. Now you can use your awareness of your breath to be more conscious of the life God has given to you.

Imagine that your inward breath carries into your body more of God's life and energy. Imagine that, in breathing out, you are removing from you anything that is draining you of life at the moment; any needless anxiety that might prevent you from believing that God is enough.

Say quietly to yourself: '*I am alive with the breath of God*' Repeat it throughout your day. Know yourself to be in the presence of the God who whispers lovingly to you: *I belong to you and you belong to me. I am yours and you are mine*

SUGGESTION TWO: Precious in God's eyes

You might focus your awareness on God's presence with you by using your attention to your breath, as above. Know that God is present with you. God gives you his life. Feel it filling you, just as your breath fills your lungs. Know that you are an unrepeatable image of God. Trust that God has created you out of love to be loved by him. Ask for what you need to believe in your own dignity and your own uniqueness in God's eyes.

You might find it helpful to reflect on the words we hear in Benedict XVI's first homily as Pope or on the extract below it that is taken from 'Statement' one of a collection by priest and poet Paul Murray (reproduced here with his permission):

"We are not some casual and meaningless product of evolution.
Each of us is the result of a thought of God.
Each of us is willed, each of us is loved;
each of us is necessary."

--O--

Statement

To be, for weeks, the glad
disciple of a single thought
has left me dazed,
yet happy as a thrush.
It is the thought that
He, giver of the gifts we bring,
He who needs nothing
Has need of us, and that
If you or I should cease to be,
He would die of sadness
(From The Absent Fountain. Dedulus Press, 1991)

SUGGESTION THREE: God in his creation

Go to your favourite outdoor place, be it a wind-swept beach or a bench in a busy city park. Look around you. Notice the colours, the smells and the noises of your surroundings. What grabs your attention? What surprises you? Remember that the creation that surrounds you was brought into being so that God could pour himself into it.

Everything that you see before you is full of the divine energy, is linked to God. As you sit there, know that the world we have been given is precious because it comes from God. It is ours to take care of, to keep in balance, to protect.

As you sit or walk around, remember also that you are unique among God's creation and that as a person you have a special dignity because God has chosen you for relationship with him. He wants to be close to you. He is with you, beside you now. Speak to him, in gratitude for his gift of creation, for the gift of your life.

Ask him for what you need to help protect his creation and to protect the precious life he has given you. Know that even if you do not feel his presence, he is all around you in every living creature and in you. He is listening. He cares for you.

What now? Paul and I stared in bewilderment into the pram and its week-old baby contents. No instructions enclosed. Home from hospital, this tiny infant was in our care and in spite of all the books read and advice absorbed, in spite of our being able to hold down responsible positions as working professionals, our seven pounds six ounces of amazing humanity left us both uncertain of what to do next. Nevertheless, baby Grainne survived our enthusiastic bumbling, and we were led by a mixture of information and instinct to discover for ourselves a few of our own answers to the "What now?" questions.

Two years later, along came baby Fionnuala, The task of parenting two very different little girls was never dull and rarely straightforward. It seemed at times as if we had signed a blank contract, our roles and responsibilities as parents to be revealed in due course. Yet for both of us, even on our weariest days, amid teething (babies) and tantrums (adults!), one thing was becoming ever clearer: these precious beautiful children were ours; we belonged to them and they belonged to us. Each tiny finger, each shining hair had been placed in our care, given to us so that they might grow and blossom into the wonderful people God created them to be. We had signed the unseen and mysterious 'parent contract', and in doing so, we had committed ourselves to loving these wonderful little ones and protecting them always; whatever that meant, whatever it demanded of us.

2. LED BY LOVE

THE NEARNESS OF GOD IN HIS WORD

I myself took them by the arm, . . I was leading them with human ties, with leading-strings of love.
Hosea 3b-4a

We do not need to be married nor do we need to the experience of having and raising children to appreciate the strength of the bond existing between parent and child. However rocky our own beginnings, we can all draw on some memories of our past or some connection with people we know; experiences that highlight the power and pitfalls of such relationships. The parent-child relationship is never perfect; limping and laughing in turns, we do what we can, trying to do it as well as we can.

Nevertheless, it provides us here with a useful signpost on our journey. This bond, this loving commitment and unspoken 'contract' that parents share with their children points us in the direction of the kind of relationship contract that developed between God and his people in the period recorded in the writings of the Old Testament (OT); a contract known better by the term *covenant*.[1]

In this chapter, we hope to grown in awareness of covenant as a way of understanding God's invitation to nearness and Israel's experience of that nearness. We will identify the words and rituals of a typical OT political covenant and consider how the same actions and words add new layers of meaning and express new depths of love when translated into the context of God's offer of self-giving nearness.

Finally, we will reflect on the God of the Old Testament, the God that Israel knew and cared for as shepherd, parent and lover. In doing so, we hope to explore for ourselves different dimensions of the experience of the God who longs for nearness with us and who, in loving commitment to his little ones, whispers into the heart of each one: *You belong to me and I belong to you.*

31

Agreement of honour

In order to appreciate the language of covenant as it appears in the Old Testament, we need first to consider the pattern covenant assumed when it became a common template for Middle Eastern treaties in the first millennium before Christ.[2] It is a very different system of agreement to its modern counterpart. Today, when neighbours or neighbouring countries have differences to settle, they have official channels to enable them to do so. However, in the broad period in history we associate with the writings of the OT, there was not an international system of law. Instead, especially at a local level, families and tribes were left with the task of establishing and maintaining law and order in whatever way they saw fit.[3] Covenant became a very common means of doing so and enabled parties to draw up binding agreements and so to establish some agreed patterns of behaviour and foster a spirit of peace and cooperation between them.

The parties involved may have been families of equal status, perhaps agreeing rights to a well, situated on shared grazing land. They may have been two powerful nations initiating the mutually beneficial exchange of goods. Covenants were also frequently drawn up between partners of unequal status, the weaker partner forced into a covenant in order to ensure the protection of (or protection from!) the stronger partner. Such protection came at a cost and the covenant invariably included a list of conditions or stipulations to be met by the weaker party, in the form of goods given or services rendered in return for what might euphemistically be called the 'benevolence' of the strong partner.[4]

As you might imagine, these covenants were so important to the respective participants that the business agreed could not be cemented only by a handshakes and a simple "See you around." Rather, the process of ratifying a covenant employed a system of both words and rituals, the purpose of which was to clarify and emphasise the extent and consequences of the commitment entered into by the new covenantal partners.[5] The words and rituals were designed to underscore the fact that this agreement in covenant was not to be taken lightly; the benefits to be accrued were vital and the consequences of betrayal too severe to risk.

The written element of the covenant listed the advantages and blessings gained by each partner if he adhered to the terms agreed between them.[6] It also made clear what each one needed to do in order to satisfy those terms and what would happen if they did not! The covenant thus included a reasonably specific list of blessings and advantages together with another, equally specific, list of curses and disadvantages. This was an agreement of honour between just and reasonable men but it also contained thinly veiled threats, included to 'encourage' each one to stay faithful to the promises made.

The faithfulness and commitment of each party was underlined and made visible in the rituals that accompanied the words of promise and threat. Animals were ceremoniously slaughtered, their carcasses halved or quartered before they were placed on the ground in front of the covenant partners.[7] One or both of the partners would then walk between the bodies as a means of solidifying, or "cutting" the covenant[8] between them. These actions highlighted the purpose of the ritual: they were promising to die rather than betray the bond now formed. Implicit in these actions was the conviction that covenant was more than a cold contract made between two parties; it was a life-changing commitment, each partner pledging his life in faithfulness to the other.

> *The promise of covenant: let me suffer the fate of these animals if I betray my word to you,*

The extent of faithfulness was further emphasised when the covenantal rituals included a meal and/or a 'blood' ritual. The inclusion of such added an additional layer of meaning. Their occurrence was generally limited to agreements between parties of equal status or power; the rituals were enacted to underline the parties' sense of shared esteem and concern for each other. When participants shared a meat, they ate together in ways that they would with family, with kin. The meal was indicative not just of the sharing of food but also of the sharing of family ties. These parties were now closer; eating together was a visible recognition of that closeness.

 The blood ritual involved parties dipping their hands in a bowl containing the blood of ritually slaughtered animals. In the OT mindset, blood was symbolic of life.[9] The blood ritual marked, in ways visible for all to see, the beginning of what they recognised to be a new life, a new relationship together. They were now kinsfolk. To the people of the time there was no closer unity, no stronger bond than the bond of kinship. Covenant, thus cemented, signalled the formation of unbreakable bonds between the two partners.[10]

We can see from the above that participation in the covenant had a variety of outcomes, depending on the respective status and power of the participants. A covenant between two equals must surely have been a more comfortable experience than that which placed a weaker party at the wrong end of the sword of a powerful overlord. Nevertheless, in spite of the obvious challenges and the air of panic-stricken necessity with which some covenants were imbued, covenant was a call to more than the rigid and fearful adherence to the agreed stipulations. It was a call for partners to care for each other in ways that made that care visible.

 Life-changing commitment

The deeper life-changing call of covenant is communicated to some extent in the choice of the Hebrew word *hesed* in relation to the expectations placed on covenant partners by their agreement with each other. *Hesed* is frequently translated into English using the expression 'steadfast love'. At other times, we see it translated by the words faithfulness, loyalty, mercy or truthfulness. Each word on its own fails to capture the profound significance of, and the invitation enshrined within, the Hebrew understanding of hesed.

Hesed referred to both the inner attitude and the outer actions expected from covenant partners.[11] We might describe the call to live hesed as a call to live covenant from the inside out, with the actions required of covenant partners rooted in their heartfelt concern and respect for each other, a concern made visible in their stringent efforts to fulfil the promises they shared.

We can see now that covenant was an honourable and binding commitment between parties that effected not only a change in behaviour but also a change in heart. Covenant was an invitation for those involved to live a new life in a new relationship with each other. Little wonder, then, that such an all-embracing experience should have an impact on their experience of another serious relationship: the relationship of love they shared with God.

> I have loved you with an everlasting love and so I still maintain my faithful love for you
>
> Jer 31: 3

The people of Israel began to see covenant as a way of making sense of the bond they shared with God. Those charged with the task of recording the history of God's engagement with his people would see and interpret the events of history in terms of a covenantal relationship with God.[12] Covenant in their eyes defined Israel; she understood herself to be God's chosen nation, a people singled out. She believed passionately that she had been brought into being - created for - committed loving relationship with God.[13] In Israel's mind, covenant captured God's pledge of self-giving nearness to his beloved people. It defined God's tender and faithful commitment to them, his unwavering, irrevocable, life changing pledge of love.

With this renewed awareness of the significance of covenant to Israel's understanding of herself in a relationship of self-giving nearness to God, we may now revisit familiar OT passages. We will hear, as it were, the familiar strains of God's love song to his people, relayed through the words of God's messengers and through the events of Israel's history. However, our new understanding will help us to hear another line of the music, the rich and deep baseline provided by the meaningful words and gestures of the covenant; melody and harmony together communicating the profound significance of God's offer of nearness, of God's offer of himself, to his beloved Israel.

You can trust me.

> Leave your country, your kindred and your father's house for a country which I shall show you; and I shall make you a great nation, I shall bless you . . . look up at the sky and count the stars if you can. Just so will your descendants be.
> Gen 12: 1-2b; 15: 5.

We can now hear for ourselves the lines of covenant playing like a harmony below familiar OT texts. Consider our good friend Abraham, or Abram as he is called before God changes his name to its new form (Genesis 17: 5) which means 'father of multitudes'.[14] In the account of Abram's story in Genesis, we find God offering him a relationship of mutual commitment and with obvious rewards; leave everything for me and I will bless you with many descendents, God promises. God calls Abram to live a life centred on God, its hesed simply stated: Live in my presence, be perfect (Genesis 17: 1b, 2b, 7).[15]

However, to Abram, the rewards are not so obvious. Descendants as numerous as the stars in the sky: these are fine words of promise for someone penning a love ballad. However, Abram knows that his present reality is very different to the commitment that God now extends to him. Abram and his wife Sarah are ageing and childless; the prospect of even one son seems to be a dream beyond their wildest imaginings.

In the text, we encounter an Abram who loves God. Yet his love has not rendered him stupid. Abram is well placed in his own society; leaving it all behind will not be easy. He realises that much is at stake and so, in true covenant style, he asks for some guarantee: *'How will I know that I possess the land that you promise?'* Abram asks God. (Genesis 15:8). We have a sense that his unspoken question is hanging in the air: How will I know that I can trust you?

Aware of the covenantal undertones of this exchange, we can identify the writer's intentions in also including an account of a dream as part of his exchange with Abram. God tells Abram to slaughter animals and to split them in half. Then, God appears to Abram in a dream in the form of a smoking firepot and a flaming torch. In this form, God moves between the slaughtered carcasses (Genesis 15: 8-21). On the surface, it seems as if the writer is simply relaying a reassuring dream about God's presence with Abram but, upon examination, we can hear that the covenantal undertones and these give richness and depth to the account.

Their significance is mind-blowing; God is cutting a covenant with Abram. In the rituals enacted symbolically in the story, God is revealing to Abram his profound and loving intentions. In this promise is the covenantal pledge of life; one life is offered to another in loving commitment. Once again, the seriousness of covenant is carried in the symbolism: *Let me die rather than betray my love for you,* God's actions proclaim to the sleeping Abram.[16]

Abram's God is to be trusted; he is giving his word in covenant to his people and, in his word, he is offering himself. *You are mine and I am yours*, God announces in every covenantal action; each ritual a sign of God's burning desire for nearness; each act, a call to respond through the actions and attitudes of covenantal *hesed*. Through Abram, God is asking his people to *Be perfect (Gen 17:7)*: God's invitation is to a life that is perfect in the way that God is perfect: whole and complete; persons united and living in self-giving nearness, in loving relationship. It is a call to live in love with God and to let every word and action flow from that love. God's covenant with Abraham is the offer of a new life of love; centred on God, living God's dream; a fuller and more fruitful life.

 ## With all your heart

As we know, God's invitation to relationship in covenant was not a once-and-for-all event. In Genesis we first see covenant appear in God's interaction with Noah (Genesis 9: 1-17) and then again, as mentioned above, with our friend Abraham. Five hundred years after Abraham, a new covenant is made between God and his people. The central human character of this covenant is a man we also know well: Moses.

> Listen Israel:
> Yahweh our God is the
> one, the only Yahweh.
> You must love
> Yahweh your God
> with all your heart,
> with all your soul,
> with all your strength.
> Deut 6: 4

When Moses enters Israel's story, a section of Abraham's people have left the Promised Land in search of food and fresh pasture and have settled in Egypt. Initially life is good but unfortunately the political climate changes; once welcome guests, these people are oppressed, often treated as slaves.[17] They need to escape and to return to the land that God had given them. God chooses Moses to take his people home.

'Live in my presence,' God's asks of Abraham, inviting Israel into a life of loving and devoted attention to God and to each other. God's request to Moses has echoes of the same deep and burning desire. God wants self-giving nearness with Israel;[18] he is asking his people to love him as he loves them, with single-minded devotion and passionate purpose. God and Israel: they belong to each other. Israel cannot thrive apart from God and God will not rest until they are together. God brought Israel into being so that she might know the joy of living in love with him;[19] living a life centred on him and *him alone*; a life rooted in love, overflowing in loving actions: nothing less would do.

> *The Ten Commandments are not an external constraint on our freedom; they tell us who we are*
> Timothy Radcliffe OP

We can identify the Ten Commandments[20] as the hesed - the stipulations - of the covenant. They convey the actions and behaviours God expects of a people living out their faithfulness to the covenant. As *hesed*, they are not cold commands but invitations to live the covenant from the inside out.[21] They paint a picture of what life looks like if it is lived with God at its centre, love of God flowing over into love of neighbour and self, into mutual respect for life and into good and generous relationships. They point to a life transformed by love; a life of self-giving and generosity; a life of loving God; a life of loving as God loves.

Loving as God loves: the overwhelming graciousness of God's offer of nearness to his people is reinforced by the rich chords of meaning communicated in the rituals Moses enacts to ratify the covenant (Exodus 24: 4-8). In Exodus, we read that Moses builds an altar and arranges for bullocks to be sacrificed. Their blood is collected; half of it sprinkled on the altar, the rest over the people.

> *Moses then took the blood and sprinkled it over the people saying, "This is the blood of the covenant which Yahweh has made with you, entailing all these stipulations."*
> Exodus 24: 8

This is the blood of the covenant. How passively we sit as these are words repeated in our liturgies. Yet this short statement, properly understood in its original context of covenant, is an electrifying proclamation of the vast and infinite generosity of the loving God who wants nearness with his people.

What Moses enacts here is the blood ritual, God's presence as one of the covenant partners symbolised by the altar.[22] In the blood that Moses sprinkles between the altar and the people, the truth is revealed: the almighty, all-powerful God, the God who created heaven and earth, the God upon whom all things depend, is offering his beloved people a relationship of blood ties, of kinship. It is a relationship offered only in a covenant made between equals. God is extending to Israel the chance to join him in *mutual,* self-giving nearness; the ties of kinship between them now unbreakable; no closer unity, no stronger bond than the bond of kinship.[23]

*Yahweh set his heart on you and chose you ...
because he loved you*
Deut 7: 7-8b

Therefore, it is in these symbolic gestures, in the deep and rich chords of covenantal harmony, that we see the good and beautiful God taking his creatures from their dusty depths and offering himself to them, freely and with lavish love.[24] Israel is being invited to respond in love to the self-giving love of God, the obedience of her people to the covenant a sign of their inner and burning desire to do the will of their beloved God.[25] God's people are being called to live *hesed* from the inside out. The invitation is to live the Law of Moses, the Torah, as an outworking of a loving commitment to God. In covenant, he asks Israel to be guided by her heart, led by love of God.

Love me . . . or else!

So far, we are exploring the more comforting aspects of God's covenant with his people, focussing on covenant as an experience of mutual self-giving nearness, with *hesed* as the outworking of covenant in actions of loving kindness. However, even the hastiest scan of the Old Testament highlights that Israel's experience of political covenants of the time loomed large in her collective memory. Consequently, an image of a God that resembles the powerful and punishing overlords of the time is never far from sight. The God of self-giving and loving nearness nestles closely beside the God of war. Furthermore, although Israel's God pledges himself to fight on her behalf, his protection and his love both come at a price. The call to live a life of love centred on God is heard by Israel as a condition for God's continued favour. Israel's God lays down the price for his continued loyalty: love me - or else.[26]

The 'or else' element which Israel identifies as part of the covenant is expressed in the Old Testament in ways similar to those found in political covenants, namely in the form of a list of blessings and curses (Deut 28:15-46). The blessings point to the obvious signs of God's favour that will be bestowed in return for obedience to the

> In the same way that Yahweh destroyed the nations that stood in our way, so will he destroy you if you do not obey Yahweh your God
> Deut 8: 20.

covenant. The curses give detailed and explicit warning of what Israel believes will happen at God's hands if she is foolish enough to be unfaithful. Boils and plague, tumour and scurvy, itch and exile: Israel expects to suffer if she does not fulfil her pledge. More than this, Israel sees God placing before her the ultimate threat: if Israel disobeys, God will bring about her destruction.

I love you and I will die to protect my love; the God of Israel swears to her, adding his unveiled threat: *if you disobey me and betray our covenant, you will suffer!* The same God who pledges love to his people, who gives them himself so he might live in intimate union with them, is the God who promises to exact his revenge on those who do not put him first. Israel's God loved and killed with equal passion. The Old Testament is littered with the bodies of those foolish enough to bargain with or betray the one true God. Friend and foe alike were wise to fear the consequences of their disobedience.

Although the behaviour of the God of the Old Testament does bear an uncanny resemblance to that expected from powerful rulers of the time, Israel did realise that God existed in ways that were beyond her understanding and outside the realm of her human experience: *To whom can you liken God? What image can you contrive of him?* (Isaiah 40:18). Yet she repeatedly attributes to God human characteristics, both good and bad. We can dismiss this tendency to what we call 'anthropomorphism' (describing God in human terms) as the product of an immature and undeveloped awareness of God.[27] However, in doing so, we also risk losing the gift that Israel gives us within her experience of God's nearness. For all his very human imperfections, Israel's God was 'real'; she could relate to him. This person-like God was personal. Israel's God was accessible; he was near to her.[28]

Therefore, the human-like images of the OT God may be flawed and inadequate but they give us some insight into aspects of Israel's experience of God's nearness. Furthermore, they present us with a God we can relate to, with whom we can struggle and weep; we see a God who understands something of human weakness and frailty. Israel's experience of God, and her consequent relationship with God, communicates something of the emerging truth of the God who longed for nearness with his people, the God who would reveal himself fully and finally in the person of Jesus Christ. In the OT images of God, however imperfect, we are beginning to see God's face.

The face of God

> Here is the Lord Yahweh coming with power . . . he is like a shepherd feeding his flock, gathering lambs in his arms, holding them against his breast and leading to their rest the mother ewes.
>
> Isaiah 40: 10-11

One of the most beautifully drawn images of God in the OT is that of the shepherd (Psalm 23).[29] To a people well aware of their nomadic past, the image of the shepherd caring for his sheep was a constant reminder of a God who had shepherded them from Egypt, returning them to safety and to rest in the land he had promised Abraham.[30] The shepherd was regarded as both a leader and a protector. The image thus speaks powerfully of Israel's experience of God's nearness to her. Israel's Shepherd-God is her shield and her strength; he is also a God of tender loving concern.

Israel's shepherd God is not the only image of tenderness we encounter in the Old Testament. We meet the same tender loving God when we are invited into OT experience of the nearness of the parent-God. This God bears the hallmarks of human parents. It is, therefore, not surprising that some Parent-God images tap into less comforting experiences of childhood, for example the Father-God of David's covenant, who offers both love and the rod of punishment.[31] However, we also are presented with parent images that put us in touch with the Father-God known by Jesus. This is the God Jesus refers to with the freedom and affection of a child as 'Abba' – Daddy - the God who is an experience of the perfect parent, mother and father.[32]

> *I have quietened
> and stilled my soul
> Like a weaned child
> on its mother's lap
> Like a content child
> is my soul.
> Hope in the Lord,
> O Israel,
> now and forever.*
> Psalm 131: 2-3

We also meet the Abba Father-God as Mother-God in the psalms. The psalmist paints a powerful word picture of Israel's experience of nearness with the Mother-God who has fed and cared for her since her birth. We can almost hear the child's contented sigh. Happy, nourished, at peace - the child, Israel, rests safely in the care of the one who created her, who gave her life. We can imagine the mother's arms as they encircle her beloved child; arms encircling a world that at this moment only they inhabit. The child sees and needs only the mother; *you belong to me and I belong to you*, they whisper to each other, heart-to-heart. Suspended in this moment their world is good; centred in and circled by the Mother-God's love: all is well.

As every parent knows, the safe cordon of a mother's arms must be relinquished and each child encouraged to move towards independence and autonomy. Here again, we find amid the pages of the Old Testament some images of the Parent-God, coaxing Israel in the same way that a mother eagle would coax her young chicks to fly. The full impact of this imagery may be lost to the modern reader but the

> *Like the eagle watching its
> nest, hovering
> over its young,
> he spreads out his wings
> to hold him,
> he supports him
> on his pinions.*
> Deut 32: 11

original audience appreciated the habits of a mother eagle. They knew that, when the time was right, she would break up the nest and force her chicks to take wing. She would then encourage them to fly by carrying them on her wings, suddenly gliding out from under them so that they might fly on their own. If they faltered, she would swoop beneath them to catch them and return them safely to the rock where she had previously built their nest. In similar fashion, Israel's Mother - God urged her to be strong and coaxed her towards independence. The same God also protected her when she faltered, catching her, ensuring her safety.

All of the above passages give the modern reader a sense of Israel, secure in the care of God. God would stay with his people, gently guaranteeing their safety and their progress. This sense of God as protective parent is echoed in another place in the writings of the Old Testament, in the image of a Mother-Father God gently guiding Israel on his journey.

When Israel was a child, I loved him, and out of Egypt I called my son.. . .It was I who taught Ephraim to walk, . . .I led them with cords of human kindness, with ties of love. To them I was like one who lifts a little child to the cheek,
Hosea 11: 1-4

Again, the picture the OT words paint for us of Israel's God is of a God of nearness, of loving intimacy, of sustained kindness and warm encouragement; this God fosters healthy independence; provides necessary protection. His touch is gentle; his subtle and tender presence speaks of a loving parent, interested only in the good of the beloved child. This God calls his people to stay close to him, to be led by him in love, to live in love with him and to trust that the love they share for each other is enough. GOD-first; nothing else matters.

Waiting on God

The passages are shot through with Israel's experience of a loving God. His passionate devotion to his people is obvious to them yet still they betray the covenant. In a long series of events, culminating in the Babylonian destruction of the Temple and the exile of some of her people to Babylon, Israel experiences a dismantling of the good life she enjoyed. These events can be understood in the context of the politics of the region at that time. However, in Israel's mind, her downfall was the result of her betrayal of the covenant she had made with God; she had defied God and now found herself on the other side of God's "Love me . . . or else!" She understood herself to be suffering the consequences of her disobedience.[33]

Strangely enough, even in their felt-disgrace in a foreign land where fate had flung them, Israel's exiled people experience God's promise of nearness as a faithful one. God's presence to them endures. Their unfolding relationship with God, evolving in this new place of exile, has much to teach us about how we can engage in a relationship of self-giving nearness. In exile, they drew on their honest and robust relationship with the God. They did what they would have done with anyone who was giving them a hard time: they complained. They loved and trusted God and told him so. Nevertheless, they also told God, *and in no uncertain terms*, how much they were suffering and how dreadful it was to have to do so.

> *How long Yahweh, will*
> *you forget me?*
> *For ever?*
> *. . .Look down,*
> *answer me,*
> *Yahweh my God!*
> Psalm 13:1-3

The honesty, reflected especially in their psalms, is refreshing. It highlights their faith in a God whose commitment to them was not diminished or weakened. Even in the face of their obvious disgruntlement, their God would stay within range of their anger; their God loved them too much to leave them in this wilderness, to leave them in exile from the land he had promised to them. Such was their faith in God's nearness and in his commitment to them, that they felt that they had simply to wait on God and to trust that he would rescue them.[34] Their Eagle-Mother God would catch her faltering children. Their Shepherd-God would protect them and lead them home.

Israel's God may have had the appearance at times of a tyrannical overlord but he was just and generous. He would not abandon his people to the consequences of their own poor judgment. Israel's God gives us a glimpse of the Abba God we would later have revealed to us in Jesus' account of the prodigal son (Luke 15). The stories are similar; chastened by the experience of exile, the errant child had come home.[35] We can almost imagine the Father-God running out to meet his children with open arms.

In opening his arms to them, God offers a new covenant to his beloved people. It is a covenant to be lived from the inside out, its laws written on their hearts; a covenant lived not as the rigid and fearful adherence to stipulations but as a loving response to a loving God. No need to enforce laws or formally teach neighbours how to love; the new covenant would be shaped in the hearts of his people; shaped by their love of God. Their *hesed* life would be made visible in the actions of loving people, not bound by Law but led by love.

> But this is the new covenant I will make . . . I will put my instructions deep within them, and I will write them on their hearts. I will be their God, and they will be my people.
> Jeremiah 31: 31, 33

And what love! The love of a parent carries something of the love of God but it does not communicate its full force. The God who longed for nearness with his people had *set his heart* on them; the Hebrew reader recognised the sub-text of this phrase; it points to the desire of a lover for his beloved.[36] A lover is exposed and vulnerable; his heart set on his beloved, he is now at the mercy of her charms. He longs for her; aches for her; cannot rest or sleep until he is with her. Such is the aching yearning Israel senses in her lover God; he will not rest until he rests with his people. His burning desire for them renders him vulnerable to their attentions, longing for their presence, hungry for their love:[37] nothing less will do.

> *My love is mine and I am his . . . on my bed at night I sought my sweetheart: I sought but could not find him! So I shall get up and go through the city; in the streets and in the squares, I shall seek my sweetheart . . . when I found my sweetheart I held him and would not let him go.* Song of Songs 2:16 – 3:4

The beloved, vulnerable in her desire for her lover, roams the streets in search of him. The God of Israel, vulnerable in his desire for self-giving nearness with his people, followed them faithfully; his ardour undimmed, his passionate desires unrelenting. *I would die rather than betray my love for you*, his actions proclaimed aloud in the rich and subtle tones of covenant and in those actions he signalled his offer of nearness in the mutual experience of kinship: no greater bond, no stronger ties.

Israel's God would not rest until he rested with his people. Led by love, he made his desire for self-giving nearness a concrete reality. In the person of Jesus Christ, God came to live in self-giving nearness among the people he loved and longed for. In Jesus, we would see God's love again honoured in covenantal pledge, a pledge lived out to the end: *I will die rather than betray my love for you.*

FOR YOUR PRAYER AND REFLECTION

SUGGESTION ONE: God's faithful love.

Use your breath as a way of becoming aware of God's presence with you. Without changing its rhythm or its pace, notice your breath as it moves into and out of your body. It fills you with life, God's life.

Spend a few minutes simply noticing your breathing.

Ask that you might come to a greater awareness of who God is for you. Ask that you might trust in his faithful love for you.

As you breathe, you may wish to repeat a short verse of scripture, a line that has caught your attention in the above chapter or one of the verses below. God's Word can become your own. Know that God is present with you in his Word.

You will be my people and I shall be your God (Jer 30:22)

The Lord is my shepherd, I lack nothing (Psalm 23: 1)

I have loved you with an everlasting love. (Jer 31: 3)

Close your prayer with a *"Glory be to the Father,"* giving Glory to the God who gives you himself in faithful loving nearness.

SUGGESTION TWO: an invitation to conversation.

God's offer of nearness invites response. Both sides of the relationship on offer are communicated in the pairs of scripture texts below. Read the words. Do not be concerned with their precise meaning. Simply let them touch you whatever way they will. Notice the words that grab your attention or the feelings they prompt in you. Talk to God about their effect on you.

He is like a shepherd feeding his flock,
Gathering the lambs in his arms
Holding them against his breast
And leading to their rest the mother ewes
Isaiah 40: 11

The Lord is my Shepherd, I lack nothing. In grassy meadows, he lets me lie by tranquil streams he leads me to restore my spirit. He guides me in paths of saving justice as befits his name. Psalm 23: 1-3

I myself took them by the arm but they did not know that I was the one caring for them that I was leading them with human ties with leading strings of love
Hosea 11: 3b – 4a

I hold myself in quiet and silence, like a little child in its mother's arms. Like a child, so I keep myself. Israel hope in the Lord. Henceforth and forever,
Psalm 131: 2-3

SUGGESTION THREE: Hopeful insistence.

It can be upsetting when we do not experience God as the loving, protective presence described in the passages above. Perhaps we are struggling to let go of old and unhelpful images of God picked up in childhood. Perhaps we are trying to make sense of a difficult life experience.

If you are filled with doubt, anger or fear, follow the example of the psalmists - no smiling through gritted teeth for them! Use the psalm below as a way of getting the conversation started; it has that heady mix of hope and frustration that characterises Israel's grappling with God. Tell God how you feel and what you are thinking.

> *How long Yahweh, will you forget me? For ever?*
> *How long will you turn your face from me?*
> *How long must I nurse rebellion in my soul,*
> *sorrow in my heart day and night?*
> *How long is the enemy to domineer over me?*
> *Look down, Lord, answer me, Yahweh my God!*
> *Give light to my eyes or I shall fall into the sleep of death*
> *Or my foe will boast, "I have overpowered him"*
> *And my enemy have the joy of seeing me stumble.*
> *As for me, I trust in your faithful love, Yahweh.*
> *Let my heart delight in your saving help,*
> *Let me sing to Yahweh for his generosity to me,*
> *Let me sing to the name of Yahweh the Most High!*
> Psalm 13

Close your prayer by asking for what you need to continue to be open with God, in the knowledge that he loves you. Believe that God's words- spoken initially to Israel - are spoken also to you now: *I have loved you with an everlasting love* (Isaiah 31:3b). Repeat these words to yourself over the coming days. Ask for the help you need to know in your heart the extent of God's love for you.

'*Guess How Much I Love You!*' Fionnuala, Grainne and I would sit, snuggled up together over this storybook, reading every page with delight. We chimed in with the words of the Nut-brown Hare and his little son, as each tried to outshine the other in expressions of love. "*I love you right up to the moon*," the little hare said one night, in a final attempt to out-do his father's earlier words of love. His father kissed him goodnight and whispered quietly into his ear, "*I love you right up to the moon – AND BACK!*"

The girls and I would make our own sport of it. Mine is the biggest, greatest love! I love you more than all the ice cream in the world, more than all the stars in the sky, all the cartoons on TV, all the flowers in all the gardens in all the countries in the entire world! We laughed as we ran out of superlatives.

The God of nearness we have encountered on our journey so far never seems to run out of superlatives. From every book of the Old Testament, he shouts aloud: *I love you more than you could ever understand or imagine, more than you will ever see or know.* This God of infinite love brought our humanity into being to share in his love, to share in his very life and even when something happened to cause our humanity to pull away from him – the distancing we see so powerfully represented in the Genesis imagery of Creation and of the Fall - God did not pull away from his people. God remained faithful, offering commitment, offering covenant,

3. LOVE IS STRONG AS DEATH

JESUS AS THE NEARNESS OF GOD

Sign me
as a seal
on your heart
. . . for love is
strong as
death. Song of
Songs 8:6

offering himself. *'I will be your God and you will be my people'* (Jeremiah 31:33): I am yours and you are mine, God was promising his people. *See how much I love you!*

> *Jesus Christ . . . is the definitive "Amen" of the Father's love for us.*
> CCC # 1065

God's ultimate expression of love, his most intimate offer of nearness, is presented to us in the divine superlative: the person of Jesus Christ.[2] Through Jesus, God expresses a love as strong as death: unrelenting, overwhelming, unstoppable.[3] Through Jesus, God heals the relationships broken by our Adam-humanity, restoring its capacity for self-giving nearness with God, Father, Son and Spirit. Through Jesus, humanity sees the face of the God who aches for relationship with his beloved people.

Jesus' coming restores our faint-hearted and fickle humanity, enabling us to once again recognise and respond to God's offer of relationship. In this chapter, in addition to spending a little time reflecting upon the impact Jesus had on the fate of our humanity in general - in terms of God's great plan, or what we refer to in the language of the Church as the economy of salvation - we will also adopt a more personal and specific focus. We will look here at how Jesus provides an experience of the nearness of God which not only emphasises God's ongoing commitment to his people but one which also heals and reassures them so that they feel able to respond in trust and in love to God's invitation. We do so, aware that what God offers through Jesus to his beloved Israel, he is offering to us now.

> *In the Sacred books, the Father who is in heaven comes lovingly to meet his children, and talks with them*
>
> CCC 104

We will reflect on the experience of Jesus as he is encountered in the gospels. As we read, we trust that we are sharing in the same experience as the early Christians who first laid down the gospels' sacred words.[4] They experienced the Risen Jesus present with them when they met together to share orally the stories of his life and teaching. They experienced the same Risen Jesus when these stories were written as the gospels and read in community. For them each reading of the gospel was an opportunity to be with, and to experience, Jesus anew.

We will have more to consider regarding the presence of the Risen Jesus with and within his followers in the next two chapters. For now, we appreciate that what Jesus was doing then with the people who met him, he continues to do now; the Word of God made flesh in him present with us always as a dynamic force. Therefore, as we reflect on gospel experience of encounter with Jesus, we are mindful that the encounter continues and that it continues as transforming and self-giving nearness. Two thousand years ago, Jesus personally invited people to come closer to God, his presence, his words and actions reassuring them that it was safe to do so. It is the same Jesus with us now; providing reassurance; offering himself.

 Transforming encounter

The gospels are filled to the brim with accounts of transforming encounters between Jesus and individuals. Here we focus in depth on the transforming nearness of Jesus to the blind man, Bartimaeus. This single gospel text is enough to satisfy our purpose. In this one healing encounter, we can see the face of the God of the Covenant, have some sense of his loving and healing touch and recognise his desire for nearness with all of his people.

The passage is provided below for convenience. It is helpful to note, that, just as in the OT passages of the preceding chapter, what we are reading is a surface story. Therefore, many of the phrases used would have been recognised by Mark's readers as 'scriptural sound bites' as it were; short phrases which adeptly convey aspects of the bigger story, the meta-narrative of the people of Israel. Reminded of this, we can appreciate that these words in Mark's gospel are shot through with the ongoing promises of God and with the language of covenant. This is another link in Israel's story; another powerful sign of God's loving pledge of himself to his people.

They reached Jericho; and as he left Jericho with his disciples and a great crowd, Bartimaeus - that is, the son of Timaeus - a blind beggar, was sitting at the side of the road. When he heard that it was Jesus of Nazareth, he began to shout and cry out, 'Son of David, Jesus, have pity on me.' And many of them scolded him and told him to keep quiet, but he only shouted all the louder, 'Son of David, have pity on me.'

Jesus stopped and said, 'Call him here.' So they called the blind man over. 'Courage,' they said, 'get up; he is calling you.' So throwing off his cloak, he jumped up and went to Jesus. Then Jesus spoke, 'What do you want me to do for you?' The blind man said to him, 'Rabbuni, let me see again.' Jesus said to him, 'Go; your faith has saved you.' And at once his sight returned and he followed him along the road.

Mark 10: 46-52

A promise kept

> I will appoint your heir to succeed you
> . . . and I will make his royal throne secure forever.[14] I shall be a father to him and he a son to me.
>
> 2 Sam 7: 12-13

The scene opens with Bartimaeus addressing Jesus as 'Son of David'. The words pulsate with promise; God's promise. In them, the Jewish reader hears echoes of God's words spoken many centuries before, words he addressed to King David, promising that David's son and heir would receive God's favour and God's protection. God's pledge to David is a renewal of his commitment to his people. Bartimaeus recognises Jesus as a Son of David, evoking memories and pointing to the proof of God's faithfulness to David's people. God's fidelity is so obvious that even the blind can see it!

The expression has further significance. A belief had grown up over hundreds of years that God would send his 'Holy One' to reassemble the remnants of David's broken kingdom, restore Israel to her former glory and mend relationships between God and his people.[5] That person was identified by many titles, but the term Messiah (capital M) was specifically associated with the lineage of David; God's Messiah would be a *Son of David*. Of course, as Christians we now know that the Son of David we encounter in Jesus is also the Son of God. God wanted his people to return to him; he sent his Son to bring them home.

So, we can appreciate that Bartimaeus's recognition of Jesus as *Son of David* gives an electrifying context to the scene about to unfold. Here, in Jesus, reader recognise God's Messiah, the one God has chosen to heal his people, to restore good relationships, to realise his covenant.

God's promise is being fulfilled in their midst; the Kingdom of God is emerging from the Kingdom of David. God is bringing about the new covenant proclaimed by Jeremiah, planted in the human heart (Jeremiah 31) and lived from the inside out; love of God at its centre, overflowing into love of neighbour; a full and fruitful life of self-giving nearness shared with God.

Keeping score

We continue to keep company with Bartimaeus. Already Mark's gospel is reassuring its readers that the God who offered his people relationship, who renewed the offer through David, is a God who keeps his promises. The connection with Israel's history reaches into the readers' present to remind and reassure; here is a God who can be trusted, who continues to offer protection; here is a God who will gather the broken bits of Israel's history and will bring about the future he promised for her.

The readers of Mark's gospel would also notice something we might miss because we have a different attitude to illness and infirmity today. The presence of the blind beggar in this scene is significant. It highlights to the early reader that God's offer of relationship is extended to all. Perhaps it does not seem to us as if a blind beggar would be an unlikely participant in relationship with God but to the people of the time, any contact with the disabled or the diseased was discouraged, forbidden. Illness and suffering were regarded as the inevitable outcome of a sinful life. The afflicted person – or his ancestors –had disobeyed God's covenant – or so it was assumed. Now, he was paying the price.

The Jewish authorities had developed a detailed and burdensome system of rules and regulations, designed to help people live out the Torah, the *hesed* of the covenant. However, rather than being helpful, the rules tended to provide a basis for the belief that adherence to rules and practices would reap automatic benefits.

The system relied more upon the notion of God as accountant than the experience of God as loving parent, shepherd king or lover. Rather than seeing obedience as being rooted in the desire to please a loving God, obedience was viewed by the scorekeepers as currency in their relationship with God. Obedience could be traded for rewards in the form of God's favour, a favour made visible – or so they thought – in a healthy and prosperous life. Those who obeyed the rules earned a 'high score'. Their account was in credit; they could rest, assured of God's favour. In their eyes, Bartimaeus was being punished. They may not have been sure what he had done but they were convinced that he had done something! Bartimaeus's account with God was overdrawn and he was now paying the price of his sin by being forced to suffer this affliction.

And many of them scolded him and told him to be quiet.
Mark 10: 48

Seen and loved

By now, it must be obvious that poor Bartimaeus's suffering extends far beyond his blindness. It seems to those around Bartimaeus that he has been singled out for God's punishment. They may even be reluctant to touch him just in case his sin is contagious, infecting them and making them unclean and unworthy of God's attentions. The people who probably cross Bartimaeus' path every day have become so accustomed to avoiding him that they gradually fail to notice him in their midst.

Bartimaeus, the blind man: isolated from his people by their perception of his illness and his sin; stripped of his dignity as a human being; unseeing and unseen.

Jesus
sees
Bartimaeus.

When a man like Bartimaeus is shouting out, *"Son of David, have mercy on me,"* he is doing so with no expectation of being heard by anyone, especially not by God. Yet Jesus hears him, Jesus sees him, and in one simple gesture, Jesus turns the Jewish "accounting system" on its head. Here, in Jesus, is the God of the Covenant, whose love is freely given, available to those who seek it, not as a reward, but as an act of

Yahweh set his heart on you and chose you . . . because he loved you.
(Deut 7: 7-8b).

unbridled generosity. No accounts kept, no deposits needed to pay for a share in God's kingdom. The only thing God asks is that his people set their hearts on him, that they live in love with him.[6]

Everyone is called to enter the kingdom.
CCC #543

In Jesus' encounter with Bartimaeus, Mark's gospel presents the God of the Covenant who was extending his offer of relationship to *all* people. No one was to be excluded; all were invited into God's kingdom. Furthermore, it did not matter if the account the Pharisees were keeping on them did not seem to balance; Jesus affirmed that what God was offering was to be offered to all and offered freely. He was echoing God's word, spoken through the prophet Isaiah: '*Come to the Water, all you who are thirsty; though you have no money, come! Buy and eat, come*' (Isaiah 55: 1).

Free to choose

We are edging our way slowly through the encounter but already we know ourselves to be in the company of a God who can be trusted to keep his promises and who offers relationship to all. Rich or poor, sick or in good health; this God is offering to all the chance of joining him in a relationship of self-giving nearness. The encounter is not yet complete; more is to happen between Bartimaeus and Jesus and it will provide further encouragement for us to trust in the God who longs for nearness with us.

What do you want me to do for you?
Mark 10: 51a

We have already established the impact of blindness on Bartimaeus. He was a branded man, punished by God, his punishment visible for all to see. Mark's readers might assume that Bartimaeus would want to rid himself of the very affliction that defined him as sinner and that he would want to be cured of his blindness. Yet, Jesus assumes nothing. He makes the offer of healing a choice, Bartimaeus's choice. His simple question confers upon Bartimaeus a freedom and with it a dignity that he probably had never known. Jesus treats him with respect. The God who participated with Moses in the blood ritual, relating to Moses in a cultural display of mutual respect, now reaches out to Bartimaeus in the same way; with heart-felt concern for his well-being; with the respect generally afforded an equal.

Mark's Jesus presents the reader with a gentle image of the God who offers us relationship. The God made flesh in Jesus leaves Bartimaeus free to choose what *he* needs. Bartimaeus's choice will determine his own fate and future. Bartimaeus's story provides a glimpse of the bigger human story and of an Adam-humanity, created with free will so that it might freely choose God. Jesus' respect for Bartimaeus's freedom to choose reminds us that, although God is aching for nearness with his people, he will not force his loving attentions upon them. God's love is given freely and without expectation; their response must also be in freedom.

> *It is, however, only in freedom that Man can turn himself towards what is good.*
> Vat II Gaudium et Spes #17

 He is looking at you

Jesus stands before Bartimaeus as the God who offers his people a relationship of mutual love and respect. When Bartimaeus is first presented with the offer, he is blind. Jesus heals him and not only is Bartimaeus healed of his infirmity he is also afforded a rare pleasure. The first sight his 'new' eyes see is the face of Jesus; God's loving attention is centred on him.

Mark's gospel account is not simply a story of a blind man's healing but is also an invitation to faith to those who read it. 'Seeing' is part of the experience of conversion to Christ. As we shall appreciate from the following chapter, the gospel community was a key agent in mediating that tangible experience of the Risen Jesus; the visible, touchable experience of the nearness of God in the life and liturgy of the community would attract converts to 'see' and to follow Christ. The story thus has layers, some of which tell the reader as much about life in the early community as about the healing of the blind man.

That said, perhaps we can imagine for a moment what it may have been like for a man like Bartimaeus to open his eyes and to see Jesus looking at him, to meet the God in whose gaze the psalmist experienced himself as known and loved. Bartimaeus; seen by the God who created him, who knew him from the beginning of time, who formed him in love, who saw him to his very core and who loved him with a passion beyond his wildest imaginings.

> Lord, You examine me and know me . . . . You created my inmost self . . . a wonder am I and all your works are wonders. . . You knew me through and through, my being held no secrets from you. Psalm 139 1,13,14,15

Mira que te mira.

These words capture the form of Teresa of Avila's favourite way of praying[7]: *Notice he is looking at you.* She adds two other words: lovingly and humbly. This is the Christ Bartimaeus saw when he opened his eyes; the Christ who looked at him lovingly and humbly, who asked him what he wanted; who saw and loved him to his very core.

Resting in God's gaze; known and loved; spiritual directors, past and present, know all too well the kind of self-acceptance that the experience of the nearness of God engenders and its healing and transformative effect. Teresa's soul friend, John of the Cross, reminds us that in God's gaze healing happens; the struggle to fix ourselves by ourselves ceases; something within us settles. At peace, open to the gentle gaze of love, we are freer to be ourselves, freer to respond in love to that source of all love. We have a word for that healing, stemming from the Latin *salve* to heal: we call it salvation: freed to love; healed that we might live a life of love with God.

> You looked with love on me
> and deep within your eyes
> imprinted grace;
> This mercy set me free,
> Held in your love's embrace,
> To lift my eyes, adoring,
> to your face
> Spiritual Canticle
> Stanza 32
> John of the Cross

Did Bartimaeus experience himself as known and accepted to his very core? Did he feel Jesus' gaze healing him? Did he experience himself a better man because of being gazed upon with such love?[8] We will never know: we can hope - and with some confidence – that he did. What we do know is that Bartimaeus followed Jesus immediately. Something in Bartimaeus had changed and his response was visible: he wanted to be with Jesus. Life would never be the same again.

> *God does not simply look at the beautiful; his look makes a person beautiful.*
> Iain Matthew

Safe and Sound with God

> *Your God is coming to save you . . . Then the eyes of the blind will be opened, the ears of the deaf unsealed . . .*
> Isaiah 35: 4b, 5

Your God is King! (Isaiah 52:7). We recognise Jesus' transforming encounter with Bartimaeus as part of the restoration of the reign of God foretold in the sacred scripture, a visible sign of the fulfilment of God's promise to his people in covenant. This is God's promised Kingdom, to be lived as covenant, from the inside out; love spilling over into gestures of love. Jesus' healing reflected the need for an inner and outer life of love; in healing what was visible – sickness and infirmity – he was also healing what was inside; restoring hearts, healing hurts, attending to whatever brokenness was causing people to choose things that were not consistent with God's loving desire for them. Everything about Jesus was a healing encounter, healing those he met so that they could live a life in a new covenant; live a life of self-giving nearness with God at its centre.

Jesus' entire life had one central purpose, to bring about God's kingdom, to restore the earth so that it was ordered to God's plan, its peoples centred on and responsive to God's will. Jesus' encounter with Bartimaeus, called by name, reveals that the vast plan of God - God's plan for our salvation, as it is called in the language of the Church - is also spectacularly personal. Gospels make frequent reference to personal

It was the Son's task to accomplish the father's plan of salvation in the fullness of time. Its accomplishment was the reason for his being sent . . . preaching the Good News, that is, the Reign of God, promised over the ages in sacred scripture . . . the Kingdom of heaven on earth.
CCC #763

encounters between Jesus and named individuals and through them we appreciate that not only does salvation heal and restore our humanity in general but that God also touches and transforms individuals, one person at a time, and in the ordinary circumstances of daily life.

Unfortunately, salvation is often described in an abstract manner or not described at all, but left hanging in the air as if saying the word was enough. Consequently, salvation can sound so vast and beyond us that it may seem as if it is something that is done *to* us, and done to us as a group. Yet in Jesus' encounter with Bartimaeus, we see salvation on a smaller scale and see it for what it is: God's offer of himself in transforming nearness. It is a purposeful nearness; in God's presence, touched by his transforming love, we are being restored so that we might give ourselves in love to the God who is already offering himself in love to us.

We are thus challenged to appreciate salvation not only as a vast movement of the whole human race towards a fulfilment of God's dream for us but also as a personal engagement, God's and our own. God's gaze rests on each individual; we are each called upon to make a personal commitment; a personal response, to God's plan, God's dream for us. On paper, that sounds like a privileged and blessed place to be. However, the reality of it can be daunting; it involves a measure of trust which can also feel like a measure of risk. We stand there with our friend Bartimaeus, looking together at the road ahead and we know that we, too, are being asked to follow Jesus on that road. The way ahead, is unknown to us. All we can be sure of is that life will never be the same again. Facing the unknown road ahead, the question surfaces, unbidden: How do we know we can trust God?

Trusting again

At this point, I am reminded of my younger daughter Fionnuala, who is very involved in sport. "Fionnuala is fearless!" her football coach told me one afternoon. And she is; put Fionnuala into the goalmouth on any pitch, and her small frame hurls itself ferociously at every shot, without a care for how or where she lands. Yet put her resulting cut knees in front of a mother wielding an antiseptic wipe and you see a very different side to Fionnuala. Her courage deserts her; she raises her hands to protect herself against my advances, only lowering them when I remind her that this 'treatment' has worked before.

In relationship with God, there is a little of Fionnuala in each one of us; raising hands to protect wounded parts, only lowering them when we feel it is safe to do so. Often, we do it without realising it, recognising the pattern months after the event. Many of us feel the need to protect ourselves because we have had bad experiences of people and of relationship in the past, experiences which have taught us to be wary of trusting others, taught us to hide who we really are for fear of criticism or derision.[9] It is understandable to be cautious; we have been hurt, misunderstood, perhaps even laughed at by others who professed to know and to care for us. In the past trusting others has led to disappointment and pain.

We bring our human wounds into our relationhsip with God including the effects of past human experiences that, for many and complex reasons impact on our experience of God.[10] Old images of God loom large, and in times of difficulty and disappointment, we seem to recall all too readily the accounts of a punishing, jealous or angry God, mentioned above. Little wonder that we inwardly tremble at the thought of such a God approaching our wounded places. Who but a lunatic would let such danger close to parts of us already experiencing pain?

We will revisit some unhelpful images of God below, in Chapter Six. Here we reflect on how Jesus provides a truer and fuller picture of who God is and offers us an 'antidote' to the unhelpful images of God. Jesus furnishes us with a consistently reassuring experience of the nearness of a God who cares for us and who can be trusted. As we have observed in his encounter with Bartimaeus, and as is evident from all of his contact with others, Jesus points us to a God who hears and sees us. This God knows our fickle fancies and our deepest desires. Nothing is hidden from him and we have no need to hide; we can rest easy in his gaze of love. The God we meet in Jesus sees and knows us as individuals. He knows what we need.

At this moment in time God's revelation is addressed not to people in general but to me . . . I must rid myself of every trace of the idea that I am merely part of a crowd going in the same direction, which might do just as well if not better, without me.

Hans Urs von Balthasar,

The God we see in Jesus has our best interests at heart. We saw it in his attention to Bartimaeus. He does not treat Bartimaeus as one of a crowd; he affords him his dignity and his freedom. It is significant that Jesus does not impose healing on Bartimaeus. We so often assume that God has a spiritual obstacle course planned to make us better people and that if we say YES to relationship with God he will sign us up for it, whether we like it or not! Bartimaeus is *asked*. God asks. God does not press himself and his healing upon us. We are not sucked up and swallowed in one enormous process of salvation but, instead, we are attended to and loved, one person at a time.[11] With God the divine healer, we *can* 'drop our hands'; it *is* safe to let him close, to hand ourselves over to him to be loved and restored for relationship.

We are safe with God; little wonder then that the Latin root *salve*, mentioned above, carries within it the *sense* of feeling safe and sound.[12] In the Genesis story, Adam and Eve did not feel safe with God; they grasped what they wanted because they believed the serpent's lie; it convinced them that God would deny them what they truly needed. Jesus came to dispel that lie, so that we might trust in God's desire to provide for us everything we truly need, that we might once again know ourselves to be 'safe and sound' in a life of nearness with our loving God.

 Love strong as death

For those of us who are still wary of trusting God, we might do well to remember God's pledge to his people in covenant, the ritual actions communicating a profound truth: *I will die rather than betray my promise to you*. We see God's pledge of his life made manifest in Jesus. In Jesus, God would show the true extent of his commitment to his beloved people, the full extent of his desire for nearness with them.

Jesus' encounter with Bartimaeus precedes his entry into Jerusalem where he knew his proclamation of God's Kingdom would bring him into direct conflict with the Jewish authorities.[13] The Bartimaeus account refers to the large crowds that surrounded Jesus. His mission was gathering momentum and the popularity of his teaching was becoming obvious to the Jewish authorities. Jesus was far from popular with these authorities. He weakened their grip on the people and he threatened the relationship of uneasy stability that they had brokered with their Roman overlords. He threatened their Law and appeared to be loosening their grip on God. Jesus had to die.

Jesus must have reckoned on the possibility of his own death.[14] A weaker man would have avoided conflict, avoided Jerusalem, retracted messages and made public apologies. Not Jesus. He continued to preach God's Kingdom to all, reaching out with a

message of God's love even to those who would be considered 'unclean'. Even when he knew that the continuation of his preaching and his mission would inevitably lead to his death, he still proclaimed God's love and dared to speak in God's name. In the end, Jesus chose to give his life rather than deny God's love; he died rather than betray God's commitment to his people.[15] *See how much I love you!* his death proclaimed.

The God who pledged himself in covenant to Israel gave his life for his people. He would not betray his word nor withdraw his commitment to them. God's pledge to honour the covenant with his life is highlighted at the Last Supper not only in Jesus' gift of himself in his Body but also in his gift of his Blood. In the OT, Blood is the sacred gift of life. With Jesus, it is a sign of God's gift of his life to and for his people. The blood of the covenant is a sign of a life shared and bonds of kinship made between God and his people.[16] Now the new covenant God had promised is being fulfilled by Jesus. Here is a God who could be trusted, who suffered and died out of love for his people, whose love for them endures beyond the grave: whose love is as strong as death: unrelenting, overpowering, unstoppable.

> *This cup is the new covenant of my blood*
> Luke 22:20b

More than you could ever ask or imagine.

If we require further reassuring evidence of the safety of God's plan for our salvation, we might look to where the plan is heading. In other words, we might cast an eye towards our destination as humans. The destination is not a place, but a person. Our Adam-humanity is moving in one direction, growing so that we become more able to love as God loves; more able, therefore, to participate in the Divine love shared by Father, Son and Holy Spirit. Our goal is even more specific: our goal is Jesus. *Christ the new Adam . . . fully reveals man to himself and brings to light his most high calling.*[17.]

We are in the process of becoming like Jesus; this is our *high calling*: to share Christ's loving obedience to, and trust in, the Father; to share in his self-giving nearness with God. *'For this is why the Word became man . . . so that man, by entering into communion with the Word and thus receiving divine sonship, might become a son of God. 'For the Son of God became man so that we might become God.'* [18]

And the result? Imagine what it would be like to open our eyes, freed from the blindness of our self-centred concerns, and to see the world with the same sense of delight as does the creator God. Imagine wakening each morning with the excitement of a child. Imagine approaching creation with a child's wonder, and facing into the day with trust in Abba-God's loving presence. Imagine feeling loved to your very core, cared for, needed, appreciated: wanted. Imagine living in a world where people took care of each other because they wanted to, where love of God was palpable and visible in every smile, every comforting gesture and every helping hand. Imagine a day when you felt alive with the breath of God, truly alive; every colour bright, every sound sharp, your joy complete.

Now you are imagining something of God's plan for your salvation; for a future filled with peace; a share in Christ's kinship, a life lived in the lavish love of God. Now you are dreaming God's dream of Kingdom.

In Jesus, we see the face of the God who wants to be near to us and we know that he is a good and faithful God who cares for his people. Jesus shows us a God who can be trusted and who has our best interests at heart. God has a plan for our salvation and it is a good plan. Through his healing and purposeful nearness, he will make us fit and ready for relationship with him for an eternity. With Jesus, God's vast and mighty plan is given a human face, the face of the healer and the face of the healed. We look to him and there we see our destiny, see ourselves restored in God's image and likeness; able to love and live as Jesus did, with passion and purpose, in joyful and generous service of God and of others; able to live with great peace and true happiness.

The purpose of this chapter was not to present theological proofs for God's nearness to us in Jesus. Instead, it was to achieve a more 'human' objective; to help us to spend some time in nearness with Jesus of the gospels so that we might recognise and respond to God's invitation to 'drop our hands', in the knowledge that the God who offers healing and wholeness can be trusted. This God came to live among his people and he died rather than deny his love for them. This God's love is as strong as death.

> *Glory be to him whose power working in us can do infinitely more can we can ever ask or imagine.*
> Ephesians 3:20

As Christians, we know that God's offer of relationship did not end with Jesus' death but instead entered a new phase. And so, we turn to another chapter and yet another dimension of the experience of the self-giving nearness of God: God's nearness in the Body of Christ.

FOR YOUR PRAYER AND REFLECTION

SUGGESTION ONE: A God we can Trust

Imaginative contemplation of scripture: A few words of introduction

In what follows, we trust in the early Church's experience of the Risen Jesus present with them when they read aloud his life and teachings in the form of the gospels. We believe, as they did, that each reading is a new opportunity to meet Jesus, to get to know him. He is with you, now. What he did then; he is doing now in your life, in your presence.

We cannot conjure up an experience of God but there are ways to help foster a better appreciation of Jesus' presence. One way, a particular favourite of St Ignatius and his Jesuits is "imaginative contemplation". The method is simple, but some people find it difficult to imagine or to picture events. Do not worry if this describes you. What matters is that you ask for a growing awareness of the Jesus who is present with you as you read.

Find a quiet place where you will not be disturbed for ten minutes. Help yourself to be aware of Christ's presence with you: light a candle; play quiet music, place an empty chair close by and imagine him sitting there

Prayer is God's work. You might begin by asking God for help to pray and asking that through your prayer you may come to know and love him.

You do not need a blank mind but it does help to feel at rest. One way of becoming more peaceful is to focus on your breathing. Without controlling its pace or rhythm, simply notice your breathing in and breathing out.   *(continues on next page)*

SUGGESTION ONE (cont.)

Read the Bartimaeus passage again. Imagine it as if you are watching it on the TV. Do not worry about what is "happening". Simply let yourself be there with Jesus. Notice what he is like as you enter into the story for yourself. Imagine the crowds, the noise, the heat, the air of excitement as Jesus approaches. Picture the blind man huddled under a heavy cloak . . . hunkering on the ground . . . or imagine yourself as Bartimaeus and let the story which unfolds become your story as you read it.

Spend a few minutes sitting quietly after you have read the passage. Again, do not get caught up in analysis.

As you sit, imagine Jesus sitting with you in the room. What do you need him to know? What is your answer to his question "What do you want me to do for you?" What might you need to 'see again' at this time?

Finish your prayer with a formal prayer: 'Our Father' or 'Glory be to the Father'

For further reflection:
What words describe for you the Jesus you met in this scene?
How did you feel when you heard his question?
What stands out for you from the prayer?

SUGGESTION TWO In the gaze of God.

Quieten down for prayer by using your awareness for your breathing, as before.

This prayer is simple: know that you are sitting in God's presence.

Become aware of the God who is looking at you, who sees and accepts all that you are.

As you sit there, aware that God is looking at you, you may become acutely conscious of your weaknesses. Know that God sees and accepts everything about you, your weaknesses and inadequacies; your beauty and your goodness.

Ask for help to be able to recognise and accept the entire person God see before him.

Trust that in his gaze, even if you do not feel it, he is making you more beautiful.

It seemed strange at the time that the bishop should go to such lengths to bring me back a children's book. He had found a copy during a trip to Scotland: *Badger's Parting Gifts* by Susan Varley.[1]   Read it, he said; I would understand why it was one of his favourites. I read it and I understood.

Varley's book helps children come to terms with the death of a loved one by encouraging them not only to grieve but also to remember all the good things that the person they loved had left behind. The book's central character, Badger, had made good friends during his life, shown great generosity and patience in sharing with them his time and talents. He taught one friend to make paper chains, another to skate, another to make a knot in his tie, another to cook gingerbread. When he died, each one cherished a fond memory of him. They missed him dreadfully but their pain at his loss was softened by their memories and their gratitude for what he had given them. They came to realise that in many ways he was still alive to them in the skills and habits he had shared with them.

We can each make our own connections between this children's story and our own lives. We all know someone who has passed on their love or their good (or bad!) habits to us. They can feel alive once again to us in our remembering their attitudes and actions. A gesture, a word,

4. BECOMING WHAT YOU RECEIVE

THE NEARNESS OF GOD IN THE BODY OF CHRIST

This is my Body given for you. Do this in memory of me.
Luke 22: 19b

scribbled note, a keepsake: all can serve to remind us of the loving impact of the person who is no longer with us. Over time, the memory of what they have left us gives us comfort. It enables them to live on, in our memories and in our actions.

 There was little comfort available to Jesus' disciples in the time immediately following his death. They had watched this passionate man move with purpose among the people, preaching with such love and conviction. They had been drawn into his vision, caught by his burning desire to make God's dream of Kingdom a reality for everyone who wanted to live a life in love with God. Moreover, they had watched him heal not only the sick and disabled but also the unwanted and the unseen. They listened to his gentle words, watched the tenderness of his touch and saw the love of God in action before them. Jesus had such a profound impact on those who followed him. Now he had been taken from them violently and without warning. What would they do without him?

We know that Jesus' followers did not have to rely on memory, but how did their human minds grasp the enormity of what followed? Many of Jesus' disciples had left their old lives behind simply because they wanted to be close to him and to spend a new life with him. What would it have been like for them to lose him to such a violent death and then to see him restored into their company in such amazing circumstances? What questions would have flooded their minds and troubled their hearts when they heard him announce his imminent return to the Father? How were they going to sustain the energy and love that he had instilled in their hearts? How were they to live without him when he had been such a vital part of their life, such a bottomless source of God's love and longing?

In this chapter, we will reflect on what we know as Christians: that our experience of the nearness of God continues in the Risen Jesus who, through his Spirit, remained present with and within his followers. We will see how the Spirit transformed Jesus' followers, inviting them into a radically new way of living in nearness with God and with each other as the Body of Christ. Finally, we will remember that we, parts of the Body of Christ, share also in that ongoing transforming experience of the nearness of God, Father, Son and Holy Spirit.

A note on language, before we proceed. The title most often applied to Jesus is that of Christ, from the Greek "*Christos*" meaning Messiah. In what follows you will see Christ used in some places and the Risen Jesus in others. No theological point is being made in varying the use. Insertion of the term Risen Jesus merely helps to keep the thread of experience between the early Church and the disciples who shared Jesus' company when he walked the earth. The Risen Jesus keeps in our minds that it is the Jesus of the early encounters; it is the same Christ: what he did then, he is continuing to do among his followers.

 He breathed on them . . .

On the evening of the same day [Easter] *. . . Jesus came and stood among them. He said to them: "Peace be with you . . . As the Father is sending me, so am I sending you." After saying this, he breathed on them and said: "Receive the Holy Spirit . . ."*

John 20: 19– 22.

Breathing on people seems such a strange action, even for a newly resurrected Messiah.[2] Not so, if we remember that John's gospel is a master class in layering one meaning on top of another. The breath is a scriptural sound bite; breathing is never just breathing. The gospel's early readers would have appreciated this. They would see the word *pneuma* in the text where we now read 'breath'. They would recognise it as the Greek equivalent of the Hebrew *ruach*.[3]

Ruach: we recognise this word from the creation story. This is the Holy Breath of God; God's Holy Spirit. In carefully selecting the word *pneuma*, John is emphasising here that the same Spirit given to creation in the beginning, a share of God's life, is now given anew by the Risen Jesus. *Receive the Holy Spirit*, Jesus says and with the Spirit, he is offering his disciples life. However, it is new life; new life in Christ: eternal life.

> *The Spirit of the Lord is upon me, for he has anointed me to bring the good news . . . to proclaim a year of favour from the Lord.*
> Luke 4: 19-18
> Is 61: 1-1; CCC #714

Jesus is sharing with his disciples the same Spirit who was so intimately present with and within him throughout his life,[4] the Spirit who fuelled and fired his own mission, stirring up within him the blazing love and bottomless desire of the God who wanted relationship with his people.

The same fire and passion, the same life and longing of God would now be theirs too. "*As the Father is sending me, so am I sending you,*" he tells them. His mission would be their mission; they would be his loving presence in the world, proclaiming to the world the Good News that the covenant and the promise of God's kingdom were being fulfilled; God living in their midst, inviting them into nearness, inviting them to live in love with him.

Although we recognise the familiar tones of covenant in the promise of Kingdom, what was on offer now would prove to be a new experience of God's nearness, through his Holy Spirit. In the past, Jewish exiles discovered for themselves that God's presence was not confined to the Temple in Jerusalem; God was at home with them in their place of exile. The disciples' experience goes a stage further, a step closer; a step within.

. . . that is what we are - a temple of the living God. We have God's word for it: 'I shall fix my home among them and live among them; I will be their God and they will be my people'
(2 Cor 6: 16)

Now, with the gift of the Spirit, Jesus' disciples encounter the God who seeks greater nearness with his people, who wants to make his home with them in their hearts. This God would be with them always (Matt 28:20b), dwelling in self-giving nearness within them.[5]

Do you love me . . . ?

The Jesus we encountered above in our reflections on the healing of Bartimaeus did not force healing on him but extended an invitation. "What do you want me to do for you?" he asked. It is the same Jesus, now Risen, who encounters the disciples. This time he asks Peter a question, inviting a response. *"Do you love me . . . ?"* (John 21: 15-17)

Peter's story leading up to the crucifixion is all too familiar to us. Under pressure, afraid for his life, Peter denies his friendship with Jesus; he betrays his friend. *"I do not know him,"* he assures the servant girl. Twice more he disowns Jesus, his earlier insistence of undying loyalty forgotten in a haze of fear (Lk 22: 54-62).

Peter's denial of Jesus is recorded in all of the gospels. This strong and burly man now weakened; his love for Jesus eclipsed by something stronger. Love as strong as death: not Peter's; not yet.

> .. by virtue of that obedience unto death hanging from a cross, [Jesus] dissolved [Adam's]. ancient disobedience
> St Irenaeus

"Do you love me . . . ?" the Risen Jesus asks Peter. Peter gets his chance to say his YES. . . and YES and YES again. Peter gets his chance to look Jesus in the eye, to pledge himself again in love and to say: "Lord, you know everything, you know I love you." (John 21: 15-17)

This closing scene of John's gospel presents a story of hope, of restored relationship, of God's faithful and forgiving love. It is not simply Peter's story but our own. Jesus through his death and resurrection offers our Adam-humanity a chance to say its YES again to God,[6] to recognise God's generous gift of himself in love, to open and to respond to that love; trusting that it is enough; that God alone is enough.

> The Son of God, Jesus Christ . . . was never YES and NO; his nature is all YES. For in him is found the YES to all God's promises and it is 'through him' that we answer our Amen [YES! It is so]
> 2 Cor 1: 20.[1]

Jesus' conversation with Peter has implications; it is not simply the request for a loving loyalty but it signals the beginning of a life of love. *Feed my sheep, my lambs . . . Look after my sheep:* love them as I have loved you, Jesus is telling Peter. He is inviting Peter and the disciples to join him living in love; he is inviting them to join him in his YES to the Father. The invitation is extended to our humanity. Do you love me? God asks, longing for mutual self-giving nearness with his people. Jesus' life, his very being is the answer to God's question and the means by which God and humanity might slake their mutual thirst. Humanity is invited to unite itself with Jesus in his eternal response. [7]

Do you love me . . . ? The question comes again.

Peter's voice sounds its reply, no doubt each time louder than the first; his voice carrying with it the voices of the early Church, united with the voice of the Risen Jesus. YES! Peter says. YES! YES!

Love one another as I have loved you

Jesus charged his disciples with the task of continuing his mission on earth. They would be living witnesses to the coming of God's Kingdom; the witness they would give to his life and love would bring others into relationship with God, Father, Son and Spirit. Furthermore, like Jesus, they would be God's loving presence in the world, inviting his people into self-giving nearness with God, Father, Son and Holy Spirit.

The disciples had united with the Risen Jesus in saying YES to God's will, in bringing about God's reign, God's Kingdom. The Jesus of John's gospel describes concisely the way in which they will live out their YES to God: *Love one another as I have loved you* (John 15: 12). The disciples must have understood the challenge in his words. They had accompanied Jesus on his mission; they watched this wonderful man, moving gently among God's beloved people; healing, forgiving, caring for even those whom society despised and rejected. They had experienced him as teacher, as leader, as friend. They knew him; they knew something of what he expected of them . . .

. . . and the Holy Spirit would help them to discover the rest. Just as Jesus had promised, the Spirit would help them to hear the voice of the Risen Jesus, to revisit his life and teaching and in doing so, to appreciate the deeper significance of his words and actions in the context of God's dreams, God's passion for self-giving nearness with his

> When the Spirit of Truth comes he will lead you to the complete truth since he will not be speaking of his own accord but will say only what he hears . . . all he reveals to you will be taken from what is mine. *John 16: 13-14*

people.[8] Furthermore, through the presence and action of the Holy Spirit, each time they met to recall Jesus' life and teaching, the Risen Jesus was there with them, speaking to them anew.[9] Every encounter was a new opportunity to be with the Risen Christ,[10] to experience his nearness to them, feel his loving care for them and to be led by him into a life of loving God.

> . . . love as God has loved us . . . this love is the source of the new life in Christ, made possible because we have received 'power' from the Holy Spirit. *CCC #735*

With the Spirit's guidance and the Spirit's action within them, Jesus' followers endeavoured to live as he had lived when he walked the earth and to replicate as best they could the selfless way in which Jesus gave himself in service to others. Their communities became places where respect for each other was paramount; each member, however lowly or sick, had dignity; each one was cared for, loved and, when necessary, forgiven. They were places which reflected the dream God had for self-giving nearness with his people; God's dream of covenant and Kingdom: a life centred in God, overflowing into love of neighbour and self. Theirs was a GOD-first existence, with the *hesed* of the covenant now re-expressed and lived out in their living out of Jesus' single simple command: *Love one another as I have loved you.*

81

The Holy Spirit not only guided them but also shared with them everything they needed to live lives of love. The effect of the Spirit's presence and action in their midst was tangible. The Spirit's creative and purposeful nearness was visible in the generous sharing of skills and gifts among members; all diverse; all given for the good of the community;[11] . . . *the gift of oratory . . . of teaching . . . faith . . . healing . . . miracles. . . prophecy . . . discernment . . . speaking languages . . . translating languages . . . in all these it is the one Spirit, distributing them at will to each individual. (1 Cor 12: 4-11)*

. . . you are to be clothed in heartfelt compassion, in generosity and humility, gentleness and patience. Bear with one another; forgive each other . . the Lord has forgiven you, you must now do the same. Over all these clothes put on love, the perfect bond.
Col 3: 12b-14

References to the life of the early communities are laid down in the Acts of the Apostles, for example in Acts 2: 42-47. While we can appreciate these accounts as possible examples of early Church PR material – Paul's letters make us all too aware of another reality, of disputes bubbling up among early followers – we also realise that these people were trying as much as was humanly possible to be truly good and generous to each other. They lived and loved as Jesus did, their communities providing experiences of real encounter with the Risen Christ.

The gospels of these communities were based not only on memories of encounters with Jesus when he walked the earth but they also captured the experience of later converts who would meet Jesus in the attitudes and actions of his followers. The presence of the Risen Jesus through his Spirit was palpable, pulsating through those early communities. Theirs was not a privatised, interior experience of God's nearness; the daily life of communities provided a visible touchable sign of the God who wanted to be with his people, in every action and activity of their daily lives.

By the same token, the attributes Paul refers to as fruits of the Spirit were not merely aspirations or interior, hidden experiences but were part of the lived experience of those early communities: visible signs of the Spirit's action in their midst. They were also qualities so evident in the experience of nearness to Jesus when he walked the earth. Again, we are reminded that, through the Spirit's presence and action, Jesus' followers provided an experience of the nearness of Jesus, an experience that would transform and convince others to follow him and to live the life to which he had called them. Through them, the Risen Jesus continued to work, his loving nearness evident in the experience of being loved and cared for in community.

> *. . . the fruit of the Spirit is love, joy, peace, patience, kindness, goodness, trustfulness, gentleness and self-control . . .*
> *Gal 5: 22, 23*

You are Christ's Body!

While we must be careful not to idealise the early life of the followers of the Risen Jesus, we have some sense of community spirit that imbued the lives of the early followers and of the solidarity they experienced, often in the face of ridicule and persecution. Little wonder that when Paul chooses a word to describe them, he uses a word associated in the Greek culture with a cohesive supportive community: Body. Paul catches this sense of unity with Christ's presence and purpose in his recognition of the identity of Christ's followers as the 'Body of Christ.'[12]

> *Just as each of us has various parts in one body, and the parts do not all have the same function: in the same way, all of us, though there are so many of us, make up one body in Christ*
> *Rom 12: 4,5*

However, the Greek understanding provides merely a starting point for Paul and it becomes clear from his writings that he is referring to an existence much more profound than the camaraderie experienced among people sharing a town or village. When Paul declares: "*You are Christ's Body*," he is highlighting an awe-inspiring truth. He is telling those early disciples

that when they become followers of Christ (in Rites of Initiation to be discussed in our next chapter) they have become intimately united with Christ. Together, with him, they do not simply resemble his body, are not only united to him in sharing common dreams and desires. Paul sees the connection on a much more intimate level; they are united with Christ himself; they live *in* Christ: they *are* his body!(1 Cor 12:27)

Paul's expression 'Body of Christ' parallels the image in John's gospel of the vine and the branches. Both emphasise the intimate union between the Risen Jesus and his followers; both highlight the need to stay connected to the Risen Jesus, the source of their life. In John's gospel, Jesus is represented as the vine; in Paul, the Risen Jesus is the head of the Body. The images communicate the powerful connection between the Risen Jesus and his followers; he is an intimate part of them; they are an intimate part of him; there is no separation. More than this, the consequences of being separated from him – by their own choice and not his - are made explicit in John's gospel: . . . *cut off from me, you can do nothing.* (John 15:5)

The human mind cannot begin to comprehend the extent of the intimate union and the vastness of the life and love on offer in self-giving nearness with the Risen Jesus. Nevertheless, in the skilful development of his theme of the Body of Christ, Paul provides the early followers with a concrete means of relating to their experience of the Risen Jesus present with them, through his Spirit, and of identifying themselves in relationship with him and with each other.

We shall grow completely into Christ who is the head by whom the whole Body is fitted and joined together, every joint adding its own strength for each individual part to work according to its function.
Eph 4:15 16

If they were all the same part, how could it be a body?
1 Cor 12: 19

Furthermore, Paul makes clever use of their newly acquired existence as Body of Christ to affirm the unique contributions each member makes to the community, each one uniquely manifesting the gifts of the Spirit, each one with a special part to play. He also encourages compassion towards those 'parts of the body that seem to be the weakest,' pressing that they be surrounded with 'the greatest dignity' (1 Cor 12: 23).

Paul is prompting his readers to make real and visible the God who respects the weak: brittle or broken, every part of the Body is to be cherished; every single person loved and needed. The Jesus who walked the earth, who reached out to Bartimaeus, still lives on in their midst; the Risen Jesus continuing to work with and within them to reach out to the weak and the sick through the loving actions of his Body.

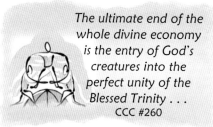

The ultimate end of the whole divine economy is the entry of God's creatures into the perfect unity of the Blessed Trinity . . .
CCC #260

Although the followers would only later come to develop their theology, the experience of unity in diversity of the Body of Christ also provided a glimpse of the union into which they were drawn in baptism: the union of the Trinity (Matt 28: 19). The love shared within their communities would be a foretaste of the self-giving love shared by Father, Son and Spirit. It offered a taste of the new life – the eternal life – of self-giving nearness on offer; in union with Christ, sharing his relationship with Father and Son, living a life in love with God.

 Work in Progress

You stupid people in Galatia! . . . Can all the favours you have received have had no effect at all . . . ?
Gal 3: 1a,4

Disputes, divisions, inequalities, bickering: it is obvious from Paul's letters that the Holy Spirit has not effected a miraculous transformation in the early communities, at least not in the sense of making individuals completely selfless and self-giving. However, Paul uses his image of the Body to provide a message of hope: just as in a human body, Jesus' followers will continue to mature; they are a work-in-progress. The early Christians thus could live in hope. The Spirit was at work relentlessly within them. United with the Risen Jesus, they would grow to live the life of love that was typical of him, sharing also in his relationship of absolute nearness to God. They would grow to be more loving; more self-giving, more like Jesus.[13]

We shall grow completely into Christ . . . So the body grows until it has built itself up in love.
Eph 4: 5,16

Paul's writings highlight the experience of the nearness of God in the presence and action of the Holy Spirit; helping followers to hear the voice of the Risen Jesus anew; uniting them in love to Jesus and to the Father; giving them everything they need to live that life of love. With the Spirit's power, they grow and mature to become more able to respond to the call to live in self-giving nearness with God and with each other. In their efforts to live a life of love as communities, they were to discover another dimension of God's presence with them, another and most particular experience of nearness of the Risen Jesus, of his gift of himself to his beloved followers.

This is my Body

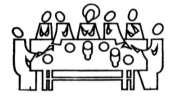

In order to maintain and strengthen their connection with the Risen Jesus, his disciples would meet on a weekly basis to share a fellowship meal.[14] They met as Jews, but when they passed the bread and wine among themselves, it was more than their traditional Jewish meal. It had become a memory of Jesus and of their last supper together before he was crucified. During this meal, they also became aware of a tangible sense of his presence with them. The Risen Jesus, present in the life of the community, was present with them now when they gathered to remember the sacrifice he had made for them.

The numbers of followers grew and their belief in Jesus caused a split between themselves and their religious leaders. New non-Jewish converts were added to their ranks. They assumed a separate identity as "Christians" (Acts 11:26), meeting together in small communities. Jesus become the centre of the religious practices; their fellowship meals evolving into liturgy, with familiar phrases and prayers. Yet still they continued to have a strong sense of the Risen Jesus present. [15]

The words used by the liturgies of the gospel communities are laid down in their various accounts of the Last Supper and in Paul's letter to the Corinthians. Each account reflects differences in the language and the experience of the various gospel communities, so we cannot be sure that we are reading the precise words spoken by Jesus on that evening.[16] Nevertheless, accounts share common formulae, not least the words we hear Jesus say over the bread he shares with his disciples (Matt 26:26; Luke 22:19; Mark 14: 22) "*This my Body.*"

The Greek word, 'soma', used here to render 'body' refers to one's entire being; *I am giving you myself*, the Risen Jesus says to them each time they meet to remember him, the bread and wine signs of the ongoing self-giving nearness of God. Yet they were more than signs. The synoptic gospels yield little information relating to the experience of the early followers as they shared their memories of the Last Supper and spoke the words Jesus said over the bread and wine. However, in John's gospel we uncover the profound transformation they experienced to be happening in their presence. The bread and wine they shared looked the same in appearance but they knew that both had become profoundly different. John's gospel emphasises their understanding of the transformation.[17] This was Jesus' real body, his real blood offered now to them; the whole being of the Risen Jesus made present and available to them in their liturgy, through the power of the Holy Spirit.

My flesh is real flesh and my blood is real drink. He who eats my flesh and drinks my blood lives in me and I in him
John 6: 55-56

In the bread, Jesus offers his entire being. His blood, as we noted in the chapter above is also the gift of himself. In the language of covenant, it is a gift of himself in mutual love, in kinship; no stronger bonds than kinship; no greater love. Here was the Risen Jesus giving himself in a very particular way to his disciples so that they could give themselves to others in lives of loving service,[18] transforming them so that they might be more like himself: more able to love and be loved selflessly; visible signs of the self-giving nearness of God in the world.

 Become what you receive.

By 200 AD, the liturgy of Christian communities had changed from a meal to a symbolic gathering where the sharing of bread and wine was surrounded by prayers of praise and thanksgiving. The liturgy was referred to by the Greek word 'Eucharist'. The form of the gathering may have changed since those early meals of fellowship but the sense of the community in celebration endured.[19] Christ's followers for the most part experienced themselves as Christ's Body assembled in thanks for his presence to them in life and his gift of himself to them in the bread and wine, his precious Body and Blood.

> Become what you receive [Body of Christ] . . . To that which you are 'Body of Christ' you respond AMEN (yes, it is true!) and by responding to it you assent to it.
> Augustine quoted in CCC # 1396

In the third century, we find a sense of shared and celebrated identity captured in the words of the theologian and Bishop, St Augustine. In his writing and in his celebration of Eucharist, Augustine repeatedly affirmed the identity of the Christians before him, linking it to their sharing in Christ's Body at the Eucharistic table. *You are becoming what you receive here*, he tells them. You are becoming the Body of Christ.

Body of Christ AMEN; every Sunday we gather, ostensibly for the same reasons as those early Christians, to celebrate and to nourish our experience of the nearness of the Risen Jesus in liturgy and in life. We gather as the Body of Christ to receive the Body of Christ, uniting with him so that we, too, might become the self-giving nearness of God in the world. Do we believe it?

Sadly and for reasons too many and varied to expand upon here, the answer to that question is that, as a community, we have lost a sense of ourselves as Christ's Body, ourselves as an experience of his nearness to others. Sadly, also, in our well-intentioned attempts to encourage "*full, conscious and active participation*" of the laity in the Sunday Eucharist,[20] we have focussed almost exclusively on the content of the liturgy and given each other jobs to do, forgetting our main purpose, the very reason we gather each Sunday. We have not helped each other to make a vital connection between life and liturgy and to see that our liturgy celebrates lives lived *through him, with him*, in him.

Although all-singing, all-dancing liturgies may prove to be uplifting and even prayerful experiences, they simply will not do as a substitute for the lived sense of the nearness of God in our lives and the realisation that our gathering on Sunday is to help us to celebrate and to live in that nearness.[21] How, then, do we become conscious again of the Risen Christ and his Holy Spirit, living with us and within us, bringing about God's kingdom in us and through us?

The Church has addressed the issue in her teaching. The documents of Vatican II, most notably *Lumen Gentium*, identify the image of Church not only as People of God (one of the Key themes of the Council) but also as the Body of Christ.

By Communicating his Spirit, Christ mystically constitutes as his body those who are called together from every nation . . . Giving the body unity through himself . . . the same Spirit produces and stimulates love among the faithful . . . The head of the Body is Christ . . . From him 'the whole body . . . attains a growth that is of God" (Col 2:19) . . . In order that we might be unceasingly renewed in him (cf Ephesians 4:23) he has shared with us his Spirit who . . . gives life to, unifies and moves the whole body . . . He fills the Church, which is his body and his Fullness, with divine gifts (cf Eph 1: 22-23) so that it may increase and attain to the fullness of God. (cf Eph 3:19). Lumen Gentium paragraph 17

As Church, we have also addressed the issue by reclaiming a broader awareness of Christ present and active in every element of the Eucharistic liturgy, most notably reemphasising Christ's presence in those assembled.[22] In this regard, the liturgy is emphasised as the work of the Risen Christ. Each movement or phase of the Eucharist is viewed as the presence and action of the Risen Christ: Christ's welcome, his healing, his teaching, his offering of himself, his transforming presence, his mission. Everything that God did in and through Jesus, he is doing in the Eucharist, in us, with us and through us.[23]

Christ himself, the principal agent of the Eucharist . . . it is he himself who presides invisibly over the Eucharist
CCC #1348

Christ has no body now but yours.

The reclaimed awareness of the Risen Jesus present in all aspects of the liturgy is of considerable help in encouraging an appreciation of what is unfolding in our lives and thus what is being nurtured by and celebrated in Eucharist. However, we still need to be encouraged to recognise God's transforming nearness in our daily lives so that we might be fully conscious and aware of that same transforming nearness as it is present to us and with us in Eucharist. We might then appreciate the full and far-reaching impact of the nearness of God in and through our Eucharist.

> *. . . the fruit of the Spirit is love, joy, peace, patience, kindness, goodness, trustfulness, gentleness and self-control . . .*
> Gal 5: 22,23

Fortunately, Paul's guidance to the Galatians is as relevant today as it was two thousand years ago. Drawing on what he describes as the *'fruit of the Spirit'* (already referred to above) Paul is telling the people of Galatia how to spot the Spirit's presence and action in their lives. When we read his words, we might do well to remember that he is addressing ordinary people. (Remember the stupid Galatians we also mentioned above!) He is directing ordinary people to look at the Spirit's action in their ordinary lives. Our challenge is appreciate that Paul also reaches into our twenty-first century homes, pointing us to ordinary acts of loving and giving; acts made extraordinary because they are united with God's self-giving of himself in loving nearness. Through him, with him and in him: we are Christ's Body.

Thus are we are invited to recognise within *us* the same amazing Spirit, reaching out through us in a million small ways in the most mundane actions of our days. A few examples might help us to train our eyes to see again the actions of the spirit. We are challenged to see the Spirit's *generosity* in our repeated offers to act as ourselves as unpaid taxi drivers for friends and family; the Spirit's *kindness* in the cup of tea or the unbidden smile. Similarly, we are asked to identify the Spirit's *faithfulness* in our commitment to the mundane routines of life, the ironing, the washing, the boring jobs which pepper and plague our days, and the Spirit's *self-control*, shown when we are tired but still make ourselves available to help others. We can also see the Spirit present in the *goodness* apparent in our willingness to risk challenging the behaviour or attitudes of a friend or family member who may be acting selfishly or unwisely.

In our ordinary acts of self-giving service, we are making Christ's loving presence in the world a visible touchable reality. When we bring our gifts of bread and wine to the altar, perhaps we can now reclaim part of the original intention carried in those gifts. Symbols of creation, they also symbolise the gift of our lives. We are placing our lives, our self-gift and small sacrifices on the altar, there to unite with the self-gift and sacrifice of Christ. In this union, our apparently ordinary loving and giving become acts of extraordinary goodness, the goodness of God, the nearness of a loving God to his people, amid the ups-and-downs of daily life.

> *The lives of the faithful, their praise, sufferings, prayer and work, are united with those of Christ and with his total offering, and so acquire a new value*
> CCC #1368

"*I am with you always.*" Matthew's Jesus promises his disciples. As the Body of Christ, we are helping the Risen Jesus to bring about that promise. We are helping others to experience Christ's presence with them so that they might know and love the God who pledges himself in loving nearness to us; the God who is with us always. We are the hands and feet of that God, his eyes and ears. Through our acts of loving kindness, others with know the comfort of his presence.

*Christ has no body
now but yours
No hands,
no feet on earth
but yours
Yours are the eyes
through which he
looks with compassion
on this world
Yours are the
feet with which
he walks to do good
Christ has no body
now on earth but
yours*
St Teresa of Avila

 ## The same but profoundly different

Over the centuries, as a Church we have lost our lived sense of our identity as the Body of Christ and confined our understanding of the Body of Christ to the precious Body received when we 'go for communion'. We became spectators, waiting for the moment in the liturgy when Christ was thought to come before us in his precious body and blood. We spent much time and effort trying to understand and to explain the transformation occurring in the bread and wine before us, a transformation often referred to in Church language by the term '*trans-substantiation*'.

The same term, which generated such discussion in the past, can now be a helpful bridge into a reclaimed understanding of who we are and what we are celebrating in nearness with God in our Eucharist. The bridge is provided by Cardinal Ratzinger's description of what is happening when the priest says the prayers of consecration.[24] As he points out, Christ himself, through his Holy Spirit, takes the bread and wine, transforming them into something that looks the same but is *profoundly different*. He transforms them so that they become his gift of himself to us in the Eucharistic species.

> *The Lord takes possession of the bread and the wine; He lifts them up, as it were, out of the setting of normal existence into a new order; even if from a purely physical point of view, they remain the same, they have become profoundly different*
> Joseph Ratzinger
> *God is Near us*

Here we can tie together the thin strands of our understanding and use the same description to capture another transformation also occurring during the liturgy. Through encounter with the Risen Jesus in the liturgy, we are being invited by him into our own transformation. Like the bread and wine we, too, are being changed. We look the same but are profoundly different.[25] In encountering Christ in the community, in his Word, in his precious Body and Blood, we are being healed for relationship, made more like him, given our chance to say YES to Kingdom and a GOD-first life and, through our participation in Eucharist and our care for each other, to receive everything we need to live that YES.

We are being built up, day-by-day into the Body of Christ; uniting with Christ, maturing with him: growing more like him. What would it be like if we really appreciated the passion and power being unleashed in us and through us because of that transformation? What would it be like if we realised that in him, with him through him we were experiencing and becoming the nearness of God in our world. What would it be like to believe the full significance of our words when we say:

Body of Christ . . . AMEN!

For your prayer and reflection

SUGGESTION ONE: The Spirit's presence and action in your day

. . . joy and peace, patience, generosity, kindness and faithfulness, gentleness and self-control . . . Gal 5:22

Recall the events of the past day. Look for the fruits of the Spirit in your life; signs of generosity and patience, of kindness, of gentleness in others and in yourself.

Give thanks for the Spirit's action in the world. Ask for help to see the Spirit's movement in your days so that you might grow in trust of the God who is near to you.

God is with you now; Father, Son and Holy Spirit, within you. Take a moment to be aware of that presence within. Use the breath again; inhale and feel your breath as a sign of God's nearness to you.

Speak to him. Know that he cares for you, that he is listening. Close your prayer with a *"Glory be to the Father"* . . . and a big AMEN.

You may wish to use a short form of this reflection at the end of each day to help you become more conscious of God's presence and action in your world. Even on dark days, something of good can be found and celebrated. If you live a quiet and solitary life, for whatever reason, you might remember the past kindnesses of those, living or dead, who have shaped your life and give thanks for them.

SUGGESTION TWO: *Meditation on the hands*

Look for a moment at your own hands. Perhaps cup them as you would when receiving the gift of Christ's Body during Eucharist. Recognise them as the hands of the Body of Christ: God's love made flesh

Yours are the hands that Christ will fold in prayer for others
Yours are the hands that Christ will use to comfort others
Yours are the hands that Christ will put at the service of others
Yours are the hands that will receive the Body of Christ
so that you can grow more and more in the likeness
of the Christ you bring to others.

Lift your cupped hands before you. Offer them to God. Know that these hands have been specially chosen to touch the people you meet in your world. Trust that, with your cooperation, God living in you will bring to fruition within you everything you need to use these hands and become the wonderful person he created you to be. He will be with you always; loving you; loving others through you.

Your closing prayer: Loving God, Bless the hands I hold out before me. May they always be open to receiving your immense love. May I use them to share that love with others so that they might experience through me your loving nearness. AMEN.

Another thought: Who is the Jesus you know, the Jesus you meet in the Sunday gospel? How can you be the hands of this Jesus for others today?

The night covers the lake in damp shroud, a head wind slicing the skin of those unfortunate enough still to be on the water. Huge waves rise from the darkness, tossing the fishing boat into the air like a tiny twig. Relentlessly, the waves pummel the sides of the boat, viciously intent, or so it seems, on shattering the vessel and its human contents into a thousand shards.

A shadowy figure appears in the distance, walking on the water towards the boat and the familiar fear of the storm is replaced with deeper dread, hearts pounding with terror as the unknown shadow moves ever closer. "It's me. Don't be afraid," they hear, the words crashing towards them through the turbulent night. Is that Jesus? Out on the lake? How?

Now the darkness is filled with a thousand questions, their troubled thoughts more tempestuous than any raging storm. Peter cuts through the turmoil with a single statement: "Lord, if it is you, tell me to come to you across the water."

Jesus says, "Come."

We see in the chapter above that an appreciation of their identity as Body of Christ helped those early followers of the Risen Jesus commit themselves to living a life of love; living as Jesus lived, bringing others into self-giving nearness with God, inviting them to share in God's life, God's love. The

5. COME!

BAPTISM AS CHRIST'S INVITATION TO NEARNESS

"Lord, If it is you, tell me to come to you across the water." Jesus said "Come." Matt 14:28

chapter above also highlights the fact that the life they chose, in Christ, was a challenging life; it called for sacrifice and self-giving. We know that the ordinary daily life of the Christian presented its own challenges. We know also that many of these early followers were ostracised from their families for their beliefs, persecuted and even killed for their professed faith in Christ as Lord.[1]

The storms these early followers faced were myriad. The invitation in the midst of it all was to step out of the boat, as did Peter, to leave behind the comfort of their past life, and to respond to the Risen Jesus' call to "Come!" Their new life as Christians would require them to follow Jesus on rough waters and on smooth, to keep eyes and hearts fixed firmly on him.

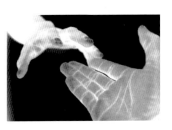

New converts marked their decision to follow Christ and to live as he lived by participating in the early Church's Rites of Initiation. The early rituals emphasised the seriousness of the new converts' commitment but also, as they were to find out, provided everything they required to live the lives to which they had been called. Strengthened and nourished by the Spirit shared with them during their initiation, they were given what they needed to live in relationship with Christ, to live a life of love as the Body of Christ.

Sadly, the sense of baptism as an invitation to lived relationship with Christ in his Body has been greatly diminished over the centuries. As with Eucharist, our awareness of our identity as Body of Christ was presented to us in scripture but the significance of this to the life of Christians in the Church has been for the most part lost, highlighted again only relatively recently in the teaching of Vatican II. This and other teaching has offered us a chance to reconnect with scripture and with the early centuries of the Church. It has provided us with new opportunities to appreciate and to marvel at what God is offering to us in our baptism.

In this chapter, we will reflect together on baptism as an experience of the nearness of the Risen Jesus and as his invitation into ever deepening relationship with God, Father, Son and Spirit. We will retrace our scriptural steps a little to reclaim from Paul a sense of what 'happens' in baptism - in community and in the individual. We will then move through the modern liturgy of baptism with the Risen Christ, recognising baptism as a glimpse of God's ongoing and limitless generosity and God's enduring and unbridled desire for his beloved people. We will hope to appreciate how the Risen Jesus shares with the new believer everything she needs to live a life of loving and self-giving nearness with God. Finally, we will reflect on the invitation of our own baptism to transform us so that we, too, become God's invitation to nearness, recognising baptism as God's invitation spoken aloud and into the circumstances of our daily lives.

 ## He is calling you[2]

"If it is you, tell me to come to you . . ." Peter's words on the lake (Matt 14: 28) speak of the human need for reassurance, for authenticity, for something and someone who can be trusted. New converts would have found reassurance in their experience of these early communities of believers. Whatever was happening to these people who professed to follow the Risen Jesus, it was making a difference to them and to the way they lived their lives. The Risen Jesus and his Holy Spirit were at work; the effects tangible, touchable; trustworthy.

Now all the believers lived together and shared their belongings. They would sell their property and all they had and distribute the proceeds to others according to their need. Each day they met together in the Temple area; they broke bread in their homes; they shared their food with great joy and simplicity of heart; they praised God and won the people's favour. And every day the Lord added to their number those who were being saved.

Acts 2: 44-47

Theirs was an attractive transformation, the life and teaching of the Risen Jesus, their life of love; all drew others to Christ, moved them to live this new life in Christ. Although, as we have already said, we might assume that the accounts of the community life presented in Acts were perhaps idealised, they communicate much of the genuine desire as well as the lived experience of the fledgling communities. However much they may have limped along in their following of Christ, what they were doing was making an impact on others. Many were converted to Christianity. Through the witness of those early Christians, many heard the Risen Jesus extend his invitation to them: "Come!"

Sitting in our twenty-first century churches with a row of tiny infants and their parents queued up at a baptismal font, it can be hard for us to appreciate the experience of the nearness of the Risen Jesus at those times when the early Christians met to formally welcome new members into their midst. Not only does our rite differ from theirs – their initiation rites often included what we now recognise as Confirmation and Eucharist[3] – but we have also lost a sense of ourselves as the Body of Christ, gathered in faith and with passion and purpose to bring another member into a new life in Christ.

Perhaps we can rejoin our brothers and sisters of the early Church - albeit in our imagination - and glimpse once again something of their awe and their sense of the Risen Jesus calling the new believers to a life of love with him. We might do so here by using historical facts about those early rites, but presenting them as a scene into which we can enter in our minds.[4] We can use what follows as a reminder of what has gone before and an invitation to reclaim what is still ours as the Body of Christ; the Risen Jesus with us, calling each one of us to "Come!"

Read the account below and let the scene unfold as if you are one of the crowd on the riverbank, jostling for a good view of what is about to happen.

A crowd has gathered on a riverbank just outside the beautiful city of Ephesus. The sun sits on the horizon, its crimson glow leaking into the blue-black sky, a promise of the scorching heat to come. The sounds of the night are quietening, replaced by the rustling of the crowd. Excitement is in the air. Familiar faces surround you, but this morning is different. You have not gathered together for the breaking of bread. This is not the same as Paul's lively discussions in the hall of Tyrannus in the city. Just in front of you, on the river's edge, Paul stands in silence, his hand resting on the shoulder of a young man you know as Callunius.

A hush descends upon the crowd and you are drawn also into this silence. The two men stand on the water's edge. Callunius, tunic and belt removed, strips down to his loincloth and is led by a friend further out into the river. Waist deep, he stands beside Paul who, with cupped hands, pours water from the river over the young man's head: "I baptise you in the name of the Lord, Jesus Christ" says Paul.

He is here.

The Risen Jesus is with you. You feel the breeze brushing your skin and it is as if His breath is on you, the air around you tingling with his unseen presence. As you watch, Paul pushes steadily against the current to bring his young friend back to the bank, the two emerging oblivious to their wet clothes. Paul turns to face Callunius, before placing his hands gently on the young man's head and saying: "Receive the Holy Spirit." Callunius falls to his knees, tears welling as if from deep springs within. The crowd around you shares a single gasp and it seems to you as if God himself is holding his breath in wonder at what is unfolding.

He is here.

On the way back to the city, Callunius comes over to you and even though you have only seen each other across a crowed hall, he says your name. "I don't know how I know this," he says and continues hesitantly, tentatively, gently. He speaks of a worry you have been carrying for some time, a concern so privately held that you have never spoken it aloud, even to yourself. "The Lord knows that it has been difficult for you," whispers Callunius, with a gentle touch of your arm. "He sees your effort. He will not leave you on your own. He is with you."

Now it is your tears emerging, prompted by a stranger who speaks as one who knows your life, who knows you.

He is here.

The early Church's experience of the Risen Jesus in their midst reassured them of the authenticity of his calling to relationship and to community. "If it is you . . ." Peter asks. The answer comes back, articulated in the experience of life and liturgy in the early Church, an echo of Christ's earlier reassurance: "It's me. Don't be afraid" Those early Christians experienced the Risen Jesus with them in ways that were visible and real to them, that confirmed for them God's nearness to them, God's presence and action within them.

[in Antioch] . . .they started preaching . . .proclaiming the good news . . . The Lord helped them and a great number believed and were converted . . . they sent Barnabas out to Antioch. He was glad to see for himself that God had given grace, and he urged them all to remain faithful to the Lord with heartfelt devotion; for he was a good man, filled with the Hoy Spirit . . .
Acts 11: 20-24

This tangible sense of presence and action of the Risen Jesus and the Holy Spirit was especially apparent in the community's Rites of Initiation. The rites involved already familiar gestures and words but when translated into this new Christian context, their effects were amazing. We may have introduced the experience as story above but the story is based on scripture and historical record. These rituals were *experiences* of the Risen Christ in their midst. They were experience of his nearness to them as a dynamic and transforming nearness.

The Rites of Initiation may have varied in form from community to community,[5] but they all resulted in the same outpouring of the Spirit as at Pentecost and with the same effect; the fruits of the Spirit were visible for all to see. The Spirit that was shared with new converts in baptism was helping them to love as Jesus loved, with generosity and compassion, with faithfulness and tenderness.

 ## The secret acts of God

The Lord helped them (Acts 11:21a); other translations render this as '*The hand of the Lord was with them . . .*'. Both versions communicate the sense the disciples had when they were preaching and when they were carrying out these familiar rituals. As they laid their hands on new converts

> *Let everyone then see us as the servants of Christ and stewards of the secret acts of God.*
> 1 Cor 4:1

and as they baptised them, they were aware that what was happening before their eyes was not of their own doing.[6] The Risen Jesus was visibly at work; they were participating in something much greater than themselves. It was something they could not completely understand, the full meaning of which they knew would always evade them. These marvellous, inexplicable mysteries, the hand of the Lord at work, the '*secret acts of God*'[7] were unfolding in ways that were somehow being made visible and real to them in their rituals and in their lives.

104

In the centuries that followed, our Church adopted a word from the Roman culture to communicate the experience of the secret or hidden mystery of God, made visible in the gestures of its liturgies. They were called sacraments.[8] They were understood to be signs of the mystery of the Risen Jesus, present and active through his Holy Spirit, made visible in the actions of his disciples; touching and transforming others, just as Jesus did when he walked the earth. [9]

What was visible in Christ has now passed over into his mysteries. St Leo the Great quoted in CCC #1115

. . . to receive the sacraments of the Church in faith is therefore the same thing as to encounter Christ himself. Edward Schillebeeckx

He is here! What Jesus did then, he is doing now. [10] We recognise the divine mystery of his transforming nearness in the seven sacraments. Gestures of love, we can see that they are invitations to experience the fullness of Christ. They are invitations to experience anew Christ's call to new life, Christ's healing and forgiveness, Christ's gift of himself and the power of the Holy Spirit.

Baptism, therefore, can be understood as a participation in the encounter with the Risen Jesus,[11] an encounter so mysterious, its effects so far reaching, that we could not even begin to see or understand what God is doing. Yet, we try to

. . . when anyone baptises it is really Christ himself who baptises. . . CCC #1088

make these 'secret acts' of God visible and in some way accessible to us by using symbols which point us to what God is doing in us.[12] We use water as a sign of God's Living Water, a share in a new life with him, a life of union in the Body of Christ.[13] We use sacred oils as signs of God's anointing, his gift of his Spirit; a sign of God's healing and strengthening touch. The white garment is the sign of our putting on Christ and the candle, a sign of the light of faith; the relationship we share with God and with each other.

These symbols of creation that reveal something of the beauty of the Creator, are also pointing to the ongoing action of the Risen Jesus in his Holy Spirit, choosing us and giving us everything we need to join with him in bringing about God's community of love, God's Kingdom. They may differ from those of the early Church but the Risen Jesus is still at work in it all.[14] Jesus' actions are visible in the actions of his followers:[15] Jesus loving, Jesus reaching out, Jesus calling, "Come!"

 ## A New Creation

The resurrection plant mentioned in our opening pages lived differently when its cells were suffused with desert rains. So it is when we are baptised. The Living Water, the Spirit present in all of creation as an eternal offering of self-giving nearness[16] offers himself to us in our baptism; [17] our YES to that offer brings us into a new way of being, a new way of living in union with Christ, in love with God.

The experience of baptism changes us; it is not the gift of something – a "grace" which can be deposited some 'place' within us and used at a later date. It is a gift of someone; God is giving himself to us;[18] baptism is our chance to say YES to the self-giving nearness of God, YES to Jesus' invitation to 'Come!'

> *The gift of God*
> *is God himself.*
> J. Ratzinger

> *What the flesh [sarx] seeks is against God, it cannot submit to the law of God. So those walking according to the flesh cannot please God. Yet your existence is not in the flesh, but in the spirit, because the Spirit of God has made a home in you.*
> *Romans 8: 6-8*

The presence and action of the Spirit within us changes us; our YES changes us. Paul expresses it as a change from *sarx* to *pneuma*. Sarx is often translated by 'flesh' or 'human nature'. However, it is not some part of a person. *Sarx* is a person who is self-focussed, self-centred, a ME-first person. *Sarx* contrasts with *pneuma* (translated by 'spirit'),which refers to a person whose life is centred on God, who wants what God wants, who loves GOD-first.[19]

In baptism, we die to the old self - *sarx* - and we become *pneuma*; Paul also refers to this as a 'new creation'.[20] United with Jesus, God's Spirit dwells within us, living and loving as Christ lived and loved. It is a new life in Christ, in God. It is an existence lived in loving union with the Trinity, an eternal life of love.[21]

> *So, for anyone who is in Christ, there is a new creation: the old order is gone and a new being is there to see*
> *2 Cor 5:17*

As a Church, over the centuries, we lost sight of grace as the presence and action of God's Holy Trinity within.[22] In popular piety at least, we chipped away at our rich understanding of grace, reducing grace often to 'graces', things given by God like coins into a vending machine, and things given often only when we had earned them or were in a fit state to receive them. Fortunately, in the past century in particular, we have managed to reclaim our earlier appreciation of grace as the presence and action of the Trinity within, changing us, sharing their life and love with and within us.

What this means is that the grace that is indentified in scholastic language as 'sanctifying grace' does not exist on its own, as a thing, a gift waiting to be handed over. Rather, it is the result of God's movement within us, firmly directing our will towards him so that we can become more like him, more able to live in loving union with him, more able to share ourselves with him. Grace is God's nearness transforming us so that we too can be like him, *partakers of the divine nature (2 Peter 1:4)*; we do not receive grace; we are becoming grace.[23]

 Grace, God's living as self-giving nearness within us, is not magic. Nor is it so powerful that it is forced upon us without our having much to do with the matter. God does not act in spite of us; he does not override our freedom to choose. The God within is the God of Adam, of Bartimaeus, of Peter. He dwells within as an offer awaiting our YES, not only on the day of our baptism when YES was said for us by our parents, but YES! YES! YES! day after day.

The invitation to say our YES is a daily event. We need God's ongoing help to keep us living faithfully a life centred on him, to assist living as his *new creation*. Our YES is also invited at those particular times of sacrament when God shares himself with us from within, transforming us; equipping us to be the people he has created us to be. We are invited to say YES to each other as Body of Christ; YES, to Christ working within each one of us through his Holy Spirit; YES, to our becoming his love for us made flesh, his power made visible; YES, to our helping each other to make visible the *secret acts* of God in the world.

Do you love me? YES!

We began the chapter by trying to sample for ourselves, albeit in our imagination, something of the Early Church's experience of baptism and its significance. Here, we return to our modern celebration of the sacrament. Sadly, the fine words of our Church's teaching are often far divorced from the experience of most of those who come forward seeking baptism for their children. Today's liturgies can be such dull affairs; well-dressed parents sitting with white-robed babies, all in well-dressed silence, the meaning of what is unfolding before them and within them lost to all but a few present.

He is here! Yet we do not realise it. God is aching for nearness with his people, his passionate presence pulsating throughout our liturgy and we do not see it. As already noted above, we need to appreciate ourselves as the Body of Christ in order to reclaim the full significance of our baptism. Nevertheless, even here when we are only reading words on a page, we can make a start. The rich symbolism of the liturgy still holds the collective memory of our Church's earlier and tangible experience of the Risen Jesus present with us. He is here! Can we use the memory held in the symbols to see him again for ourselves?

Perhaps we can draw on what is being made visible to us in the symbols to tap into that deep vein of past and present experience. We do so by moving our way through a baptism liturgy in the company of a new (adult) believer, recognising the Risen Jesus at work in her and in the community that welcomes her. We will reflect sequentially on each separate element of baptism. However, we proceed with the awareness that any sacrament is more than the sum of its component parts. Therefore, we would do well to avoid notions that any signs or symbols have power on their own to do what the Risen Jesus is doing in the liturgy as a whole.[24] Jesus Christ is the meaning of the symbols.[25] It is the Risen Jesus, through his Holy Spirit,[26] who gathers the entire liturgy and the community, drawing it into his extravagant and ongoing gesture of love.

What do you want?

The new believer approaches the doors of the church with nervous anticipation. The doors open to reveal faces of friends and family, of neighbours and smiling strangers. He is here! She looks around at the people assembled in the Church and sees the Risen Jesus. This is his Body welcoming her,[27] the community around her now gathered as a visible sign of the community to which she will belong, the place where she will find herself growing in love of God and of others. Together they will be committed to supporting each other, to living a radically new life of love: a life in love *with him*.[28]

> *Body of Christ . . .all parts of one another*
> CCC #1267
> Eph 4: 25

She walks into the Church to be surrounded by this community, the Body of Christ. The people are all around her but she knows that he sees her; he knows her; he cares for her. Today, God's vast and mighty plan of salvation has a human face and it is her face; the Risen Jesus is reaching out to her in healing and mercy, in tender compassion; inviting her to join him in his relationship with the Father. She knows that he does not regard her as a nameless face in the crowd and in the priest's question to her, 'What name do you want?' she hears Jesus calling her by *her* name: 'Anna. Welcome.'

> *Do not be afraid, I have redeemed you, I have called you by your name, you are mine.*
> Isaiah 43:1

 What do you want?[29] The Risen Jesus speaks now to her as he did to Bartimaeus. He does not force himself upon her; this is her choice today.[30] Yet her heart has heard his call long before this moment.[31] From the moment of her creation, Father, Son and Spirit have been living within her, present as an eternal invitation to participate in their loving community of Trinity; present as an offer of God's own life. Today Anna gets her chance to hear God's offer spoken aloud, in this community. Now is her chance to say aloud her YES to that offer. She hears herself say "Faith," but, silently, her heart is already making its own reply. "What do you want me to do for you?" It hears the Risen Jesus sigh into the depths of her being. Her heart pounds out its own response: "I love you and I want to be with you." The Risen Jesus offers Anna relationship and she has given her "YES!"

He makes the sign of the cross on her head.[32] Her heart hears the words God has whispered in love across the ages: "*I will be your God and you will be my people.*"[33] Here is the God who pledged his word in covenant, who gave his life as a sign of the New Covenant with his people; who surrendered his life rather than deny his great love for them. The cross on her forehead is made as a reminder of that love: strong as death; overwhelming, relentless, unstoppable. *I am yours and you are mine:* he whispers. She hears it and knows that she will never be the same again.

Anna hears his voice again, this time in sacred scripture and he is present to her anew, through his Holy Spirit, revealing in his Word the dreams God has for her; sharing himself with her, wanting her to come to know and to love him more and more. "*I am here,*" he is saying softly into the silence. "*I love you. I give my Word to you, and in my word, I give you myself. Come!*"

He is here! The same Christ who brought Peter out of the boat on that stormy night now is asking Anna to leave the "boat" of her own smaller world and join him in his fuller and more fruitful life. Leaving the boat and walking on water towards Jesus in this radically new life takes trust. Jesus' questions posed to Peter are now silently spoken into Anna's heart: "*Who do you say I am? Do you love me?*"(Mark 8:29; John 21:16)

Anna's voice chimes with the community and together they restate their baptismal commitment. Her mind affirms this *Credo* but her heart expresses it differently: I love you; I trust you; I want to share this new life with you.[34]

Come! The Risen Jesus calls her and inwardly her whole being moves towards him to be filled with his Spirit. Those assembled see the water poured on her and hear the priest's words of baptism, "*I baptise you in the name of the Father and of the Son and of the Holy Spirit. AMEN.*" However, in the wordless depths of her entire self the Spirit is at work. This Living Water is pouring God's love into her heart,[35] restoring the damage done by the sin of a selfish humanity; enabling her once again to trust that God alone is enough.[36] Anna has given her YES to Christ in baptism and his presence within her, through his Holy Spirit, heals the sad-self of her broken humanity; here now is the chance of a fresh start, a new life with him; a new life in him.[37]

The Living Water transforms Anna's entire being in ways that she cannot feel but will notice in the years to come in her actions and attitudes. Now, open to the Spirit, united with the Risen Jesus, she is becoming a new creation,[38] *pneuma*, so that she can live a life of love with him: a fuller and more fruitful life. All her desires, like compass needles freed to move where they must, will face their true north, centred now on God. The Risen Jesus is visible here in this liturgy, an extravagant gesture of self-giving nearness, an invitation to participate in the secret works of God.[39]

He is here! Anna was created to love and be loved by him and now she is fulfilling God's dream for her. She receives in baptism everything she needs for a life of loving nearness with Christ. The gifts are made visible. In the anointing with oils, Anna sees Christ giving her his Spirit. This Spirit is sharing with her his passion to do the will of God. The Spirit is

> . . . Through Baptism we are formed in the likeness of Christ . . . . He fills the Church, which is his body and his fullness, with his divine gifts (cf. Eph 1: 22-23) so that it may increase and attain to the fullness of God.
> cf. Eph 3:19 Lumen Gentium #7

sharing with her everything she needs to be in love with Christ and with the Father: the courage, the knowledge and wisdom she will need to know and to love him, to marvel at his presence with her and to live her life of love with him.[40] The Risen Jesus gives her what she needs to join with him and to become a person of prayer of love and of service.[41]

> I am alive; yet it is no longer I, but Christ living in me.
> Gal 2:20

The Risen Jesus has touched Anna in ways made visible by the symbolism and through the words of the sacrament. She will never be the same again. United with him, she is becoming more like him. Her heart beats out its new identity, echoing the words of another convert who spoke with such passion of his love of Christ: Not I now, but Christ. The candle is lit as a reminder of his faithful presence in her life; he is with her always. She leaves the Church and he comes with her; the Christ who says to Zacchaeus "I am to stay at your house today," (Luke 19:5) whispers again to Anna words heard in the depths of her heart: I want us to spend this day and every day together.

Later, when Anna visits her elderly mother after the liturgy, she knows that she is not alone. Christ is there with her, her hands now his hands, her heart now his heart. So, when her mother wakens from the prison of the sick-bed in which she has spent so many hours since her stroke, it is Christ who wipes her face, Christ who holds her hand and Christ who changes her soiled and dampened sheets. Then, when evening comes and she finds it difficult to fall asleep, it is Christ who is with her, too; stroking her hair, just as her own mother did when she was little and scared of the dark. She is scared now; the darkness of her own pain and paralysis drawing in upon her; but Christ is there, Anna's voice is his voice: "It's OK, I'm here. I wouldn't leave you on your own."

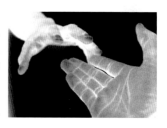

 Being Christ's Body

Baptism is an invitation into a lifetime of mutual and self-giving nearness with God, Father, Son and Spirit. "Come!" the Risen Jesus calls, awaiting our response. This is no wishy-washy blessed-bliss existence into which we are invited by the Risen Jesus – something to salve the soul for the life hereafter.[42] Rather, it is a get-out-of-the-boat call to live the rugged reality of love now amid the choppy seas of daily life.[43] It is a call to enable that love to bear fruit, an invitation to grow more like the Risen Jesus, to be his Body, bring his love into the world.[44] Like Paul, we are called to grow into Christ so that we might also be able to say: "... it is no longer I, but Christ living in me".

Unfortunately, our notions of what it means to "be" Christ's body can still be distorted and unrealistic. We so often see the Risen Jesus depicted in 'holy pictures' and, however useful they may be as inspiration for our prayer, we forget that he did not spend his time looking at people with arms outstretched and eyes raised in reverence to heaven. Instead, he probably used very normal and recognisable gestures: the tenderness of his gaze; his gentle touch; the mischievous twinkle in his eyes: all would have communicated his loving concern for those around him. Such normal human touches were so important.

Those who followed Jesus did not leave their old lives behind for a message, as if a good message alone would be enough to convince them. They chose the company of a *man*; a passionate, tender, generous man whose words of loving kindness were undoubtedly evident in every gesture, in every glance, in every touch; all visible signs of the kind of love that attracted people to follow him . . . and the kind of love that left them free to walk away.

We are asked to share in Christ's mission and to bring others into relationship with him. As God's 'chosen people' we are not given the honour of being God's 'exclusive people.' God will always do what he will; we know that God's loving actions are not confined to our Church or to our liturgies.[45] Nevertheless, we have been chosen by God. Jesus' life of love attracted others to him; united with him in his Body. We have been chosen to be God's 'attractive people' and to make God's life of love and God's invitation to relationship visible for all to see.

It is plain that you are a letter from Christ . . . written not with ink but with the Spirit of the Living God .

Be God's attractive people! This sounds so much more accessible than a call to mission worded in terms such as "Go out into the whole world and proclaim the Good News!" Yet the two statements are closely linked; the Good News is simply put: "He is here!" As God's attractive people, we are invited to be evidence of – or at least clues to – God's self-giving nearness in the world. At the end of the day, what this means is that although fine words express something of God's loving and self-giving nearness, it is in our actions that we will give attractive and compelling witness to our belief: "He is here!"

What this means for our understanding of baptism is that we see ourselves called not only to 'receive' baptism but also to 'become' baptism. We become what we see happening before us in the baptism liturgy: Christ's welcome; Christ's healing and support; Christ's forgiveness; Christ's love. We do as Christ did; in a thousand daily gestures of love we draw people closer in love to the source of all love; one small gesture at a time. These small gestures can assume a greater significance in the wider context of our call to be God's attractive people.[46]

It is only when a person's love becomes manifest in some appealing gesture . . . that I personally become confronted with his love for me . . . This is what sacraments are: the God-man's expression of love – with all its consequences.
Edward Schillebeeckx

United with the Risen Jesus, we are God's telling and appealing gestures in the world. Through our actions, others will find themselves confronted with the love of God. Sharing in the sacrament of baptism, we become God's sacrament; visible signs of the mystery of God's self-giving nearness in the world. Sharing in his invitation to love, we become that invitation: God's attractive people; signs of his self-giving nearness, his love and longing in our midst.

Together with the Risen Jesus, we are called to build a Body that will be for others the experience of the nearness of God in the world. The Risen Jesus remains faithfully with us, his Spirit there to empower and to guide us. Through the Spirit, he is encouraging us to let go of any old life that we still cling to, so that we might embrace fully the new life he offers in union with himself. He gives us himself in Eucharist to sustain us in these difficult times ahead. Reaching out to us in the gestures of love in the sacraments, the Risen Jesus, through the Holy Spirit, helps us to rise to the challenge of being God's attractive people; helping us to grow so that we might become more and more like him; his nourishment, his forgiveness, his healing in the world.

"If only you knew what God is offering . . ." (John 4: 10a). Everything that God has done, everything that God is doing now and everything that God will do in the time to come: all converging in Christ and in baptism. Shaky creatures though we may be, we are being invited to participate in this divine spectacle which is unfolding before us in baptism. It is a spectacle of wondrous proportions, set in motion from the beginning of time by a God of prodigal generosity; a God who invites us into his dream and calls us to be his loving gestures in the world. God longs for our YES so that he might give, again and again, the YES he gave so freely to us when he created us to be loved: YES to loving us; YES to a life of love with us; YES to an eternity of self-giving nearness with us. YES! YES! YES!

"Come!" He shouts.

Yet still we wait; white-robed babies in arms; in well-dressed silence. *If only we knew . . .*

FOR YOUR PRAYER AND REFLECTION

SUGGESTION ONE: Gestures of love

"It is only when a person's love is manifested in some telling and appealing gesture . . . that I become personally confronted with his love for me . . . that is what sacraments are: the God-man's expression of love – with all its consequences." Schillebeeckx[1]

Where do you see gestures of love in the actions of your family or friends? What might they be revealing to you about the God who is present with you, reaching out in love to you in the actions of others?

Where have you seen or been a gesture of: the welcoming Christ; the encouraging Christ; the supportive Christ; the compassionate Christ; the patient Christ; the joyful Christ; the faithful Christ; the listening Christ; the healing Christ?

God is here with you now. Can you bring your thoughts to him in prayer? Tell him how you feel about the gestures you notice in your life . . . or the gestures you dearly wish were there. You may wish to spend some time reading Psalm 130, imagining yourself to be held safely in God's embrace. This is the God who has held you since your baptism. He is holding you now.

SUGGESTION TWO: Living your baptism each day

It is a good idea to begin each day by remembering that you are God's nearness in the world. Whether your day is filled with activity, rest, or the necessary inactivity forced upon you by sickness or circumstances, you are an important gesture of a loving God who acts, listens and prays for his people.

Dedicate your day quite simply using that powerful prayer we take for granted because we tend to use it to "bookend" other longer prayers.

"In the Name of the Father and of the Son and of the Holy Spirit."

Let it help you to remember that you live your entire day in God's presence. Each day will present its own opportunity to be a gesture of God's love; a visible sign of a sacred reality; sacrament.

One way of making our new life of our baptism a concrete reality, especially amid the seemingly mundane circumstances of modern daily life, is to consider the ways in which we use water in acts of loving, self-giving concern for others: in washing, in cooking, in cleaning, in work, in play. Think about it: every dish washed, every car cleaned, every drink served, every baby fed; all expressions of love (even though they may not feel like it!); all signs of the nearness of a loving God in the world. He is here.

> *Glory be to him whose power working*
> *in us can do infinitely more than*
> *we could ever ask or imagine.*
> Ephesians 3: 20

A few years ago, I attended a course on liturgy in Dublin given by Sr. Sheila O'Dea. It was a wonderful experience. Every day we celebrated the Liturgy of the Word in a different way, the gospel followed by words or music to help us to connect in a personal way with its message. On the third day of the course, I was sitting in the group, waiting; my eyes closed. Nothing happened; no sound, no music. I was content to sit in silence, thinking how good it was to be given the space to soak in the gospel.

It was only later that I realised that there had not been a space after the homily. This fact dawned on me when other group members started to talk about how the movement had affected them. Movement? What movement? It transpired that I had sat, eyes closed, while two dancers had moved silently in the centre of the room; the hand of one of them just skimming my nose. I was entirely oblivious to their dance.

In this particular situation, I did not feel as if I had missed something essential to my spiritual well-being; the silence satisfied. Yet, afterwards, the memory of the experience evoked other memories; of times when I had sat, eyes closed in prayer; sat in silence. Other people told me that something was happening in my prayer but I had no sense of it. Far from satisfying, the silence served only to heighten my sense of loneliness. If God was moving, if God was present, I was oblivious to him.

THE NEARNESS OF YOU

Come then, my beloved, . . . hiding in the clefts of the rock, . . . show me your face . . .
Song of Songs 2: 13,14

Sadly, in the case of prayer, sitting in an empty silence can leave us feeling left out or doubting our relationship with God. We see others in prayer and imagine that they are experiencing the warmth and comfort of God's nearness to them. We assume that we, too, might experience the nearness of God differently – if only we could get prayer 'right'.

In what is the penultimate chapter of a book highlighting the nearness of God, it may seem a self-defeating exercise to turn our thoughts to those periods of time, often long periods, when it seems as if God is far away and perhaps even absent. However, these experiences occur more frequently than we might imagine. Indeed, it is possible that some of us reading this book - reassuring us of God's nearness - still return to our times of private prayer and feel as if we are on our own. The God of self-giving nearness is not near to us . . . or so it seems.

This book opened with a reminder that we cannot engineer experiences of God. God will be God: always mystery; always beyond our wildest imaginings; always beyond our control. We can undertake as many prayer exercises as we like but they will not create some 'perfect' experience of prayer. They do not need to. Prayer is already 'happening' in us; the Holy Spirit is praying unceasingly,[1] the Holy Breath of God moving its gentle way through our lives. Anything we do in prayer is merely a participation in the prayer that God has already initiated; the ongoing and eternal prayer of the Spirit.

Right from the beginning,
prayer has already begun
before I do anything.
From the moment
when I received the life of God
in baptism, prayer has been poured
into my heart with the Holy Spirit.
...it is the Holy Spirit
who celebrates
an unceasing liturgy,
who makes the voice of Christ
my voice,
who lifts me up
before God.
Andre Louf

Yet there are ways of being in prayer that can help us to experience it as meaningful; personal, intimate; ways to help us to trust in, and perhaps even have a greater sense of, God's nearness to us. In this chapter, we will reflect on how we might do this by making prayer as authentic and personal for ourselves as possible. While the suggestions are based on decades, if not centuries, of sound spiritual guidance, most will be familiar to most of us. What follows is therefore not new but it may be that it would help us to be reminded of it now, at this particular point of our relationship with God.

 Finding a coat that fits

We start in a place that seems so obvious it might hardly be worth mentioning. Yet, for those of us who work in spiritual direction or parish formation, it is a commonly expressed concern. Good people are languishing in the darkness and frustration of prayer that no longer gives them comfort. They rehearse words that now hold little meaning for them and fear that they are losing their faith. Frequently they force themselves  to sit in the quiet or to attend groups where everyone else seems to be deeply connected to God in prayer; in harmony with a God who occupies every corner of the room except their own.

Ask these people how they would feel about putting on the coat they wore at school and the answer would be immediate; even if they could find it, the coat would be too small; they had long since outgrown it! It would not suit; it does not fit. Yet suggest that the same logic be applied to their chosen method of prayer and be met with blank expressions; they simply had not thought it was possible or necessary to change the habits of a lifetime.

The prayers we were given as children served us well. They helped us to pray together with family and with the parish community. They gave us a structure and a much-needed routine. Their familiarity might also have given us reassurance in a changing turbulent world; the prayers stayed the same; God at least was consistent and dependable. These same prayers may serve a similar function for us as adults. They provide stability in a shaky world, something familiar and dependable. However, stability for some can be stagnation for others and some of us may need to look again at the way we are praying. Our prayer is an expression of our intimate relationship with God; our own particular way of tuning into the Spirit praying within us. Prayer is not a handbag. One size does not fit all. Prayer needs, for part of the time at least, to reflect our own uniqueness, our own personality.

It follows that if we are gregarious and find energy in being with people, then praying alone just will not do. For the same reason, if we love quiet stretches on our own and feel rested when we have taken time to be away from others, then praying in a group will not satisfy. The same logic applies to our need to pray indoors, to pray when we are working, to pray through activity. Prayer needs to be a good 'fit' for us.

Like a coat, the style of our prayer may also change according to the seasons. Our life has different phases, some comforting, others less so. Each phase invites its own form of expression. Different seasons of our lives overlap and reoccur, each time requiring different approaches. One helpful way of looking at how prayer might adapt to life's changing seasons is to structure our thoughts using ideas from a theologian called Friedrich von Hugel.[2] He identifies three elements of faith; each one a necessary part of the faith experience, each one present in varying proportions over a life-time.' Adapting his language to suit a modern audience,[3] we can use von Hugel's categories to help us to understand something of our changing experiences of, and needs, in prayer.

Firstly, in our prayer there is an element of **security**. This is represented in the formal prayers we learn, the comforting and familiar rituals and liturgies in which we participate at home and in Church. Secondly, there is an element of **searching**. This takes the form of the conversations we have with God, the psalms of struggle and anger, the space given over to questioning, to reading and discussion; to learning about God. Finally, there is an element of **intimacy.** This is represented by the part of our prayer that is an experience of God present with us, or, at least, helps foster such awareness. The music, candles and incense of our liturgies; silence shared; scripture, people; places; all contribute to the element of intimacy, that sense, however fleeting or elusive, that the God to whom we pray is with us now.

Searching

Security

Intimacy

These elements assume a different priority at different stages of life and we might guess at the general pattern that develops over a lifetime. A child's prayer will have a greater emphasis on security, a teenager's on searching and an adult's on intimacy. However, life is complex; the pattern is rarely experienced in such a tidy and predicable fashion. Life's challenges, God's mystery, our own painful growth and development; all can throw us on choppy waters. The element of security in our prayer can quickly be outweighed by the element of searching. The felt-sense of intimacy ebbs and flows. Our prayer changes with life's seasons.

This search for a way of praying that is a "good fit" - a way of praying that changes over time and that suits our personality - may sound a little self-indulgent and even unnecessary. After all, the Holy Spirit is, doing the work of prayer within us. Prayer is God's initiative not ours. Nevertheless, God's initiative always invites our response and, in intimate relationship, that response needs to be personal, unique, particular. Finding a coat that fits helps us to make our own unique response to the God who has called each one of us by name and who knows and relates to each one as individual. It helps us to find our particular voice, our own way of talking to God and of being with God. It helps us to discover a God who wants to be with us, who not only loves us but who actually *likes* us and likes spending time in prayer with us – wherever we choose to take him, be it to the park for a walk or into a dark room for some quiet time together.

God in the good room

In my Father's house there are many rooms, we hear Jesus say in John's gospel (John 14:2) but we might wonder if we have given much thought to the rooms in our lives to which we give God access. Think of it in this way: many of us have one room in the house that we try to keep as tidy as possible so that when we have visitors – the great aunt Elsie's of the world who come as pleasant but infrequent guests – we do not have to clear a space for them to sit down. Instead, we bring them into this 'good' room, give them our best tea in our best cups and try as best we can to make polite conversation. Only the respectable fragments of our lives are put on display, not because we consciously fear criticism but, rather, we assume that great aunt Elsie's of the world did not visit to listen to our troubles. We treat our guests as one would treat good china; handling them carefully to avoid breakage.

There are times when we relate to God in the same way as we do to great aunt Elsie. The various parts, the different 'rooms' of our life, may be in disarray as life throws its difficulties in our direction. Yet still we sit with God in a 'good room', the words of our prayer straining between us like polite conversation. We smile sweetly; ask God nicely for what we think we might need and wait in a very grateful and well-behaved fashion for his response. The good room conversation is well intentioned; skilfully choreographed: we handle God carefully to avoid breakage.

Our relationship with the aunt Elsie's of our lives may be pleasant enough but could hardly be described as fulfilling. Certainly, if we were in the midst of a crisis it is unlikely that poor Elsie would have much chance to hear about it and to lend support. Our conversation instead is an experience of polite distance. We are there with each other but not there for each other; sitting together, we are miles apart.

We can be forgiven for behaving in this way with God. For centuries, we have quietly separated the 'holy' from the ordinary, carefully installing God in the good rooms of Church and tabernacle. We are not used to relating to the God who would be just as happy to take a seat at our kitchen table, and to be there for us in the midst of life's mess. Furthermore, as a Church, we have actively encouraged polite conversation with God, fostering the unspoken belief that we have to be 'nice' in God's company, that our stance before him must be one of gratitude and unwavering trust.

> To the question, "God, what is your will for me?" the answer is understood to be, "I want you to be yourself. I leave the details of that up to you."
> Thomas Hart

Such expectations place unnecessary and unhelpful demands on our prayer. We are invited into intimacy with God; intimacy is based on a relationship of openness and honesty. The invitation of intimacy is to be open, to "Be yourself!" with the God who cares deeply for you, who loves you as you are. Putting God in the good room can have its impact on this intimacy. It is hard to be yourself in the good room. The God we have placed in there can seem very far away.

Again, it is helpful to remind ourselves that the God we encounter in Jesus did not visit good rooms nor did he confine himself to the more typical sacred and holy places of his time. He dined with sinners and tax collectors. He ate with friends, probably spending much of his time listening to their problems as well as their joys. This God will feel at home in the kitchen places of our lives[4] and in the messy corners that we try to hide from him and from ourselves. An extra mug of tea and an empty seat at the table may be all we need to be prompted to be ourselves, to let him into every room in the house and to experience him not only there with us but there for us.

An Angry God

Before we become too enthusiastic about being free to be ourselves before God, we might do well to admit that in the past we felt we had good reason to confine God to the good room. The images we had of God, the ideas picked up from others: all of these added to our doubts and concerns about letting God enter the messier kitchen places of our lives. Created for love, destined for relationship; we are born wanting God. Yet our early experiences may have twisted us out of shape. The past has marked us and more subtly than we might imagine.[5]

Relationships may have impacted on us in the past. Some of the people we allowed close to us may have treated us badly and in ways that significantly influenced our willingness to let God close also. Perhaps we have risked showing such people the kitchen places of our lives; places that were messy and disorganised: our troubles at work, our struggles with family members; our fears and inadequacies. Sadly, we discovered to our cost, that our trust in them was misplaced. They looked at the exposed disorder of our lives and found us wanting. They criticised our words and actions and at some very deep level, either intentionally or unintentionally, they hurt us.

However much we may have tried to shrug off their criticism, some of it may have pierced the skin. The pain has taught us about the dangers of trusting others and letting them "in". Consequently, we may have learnt that it is wiser to keep most people, including God, at a safe distance – out of the kitchen and in the good room instead.

Added to any pain from past hurts is the Church's collective memory of a critical and harsh God. The memory lingers, especially in the minds of the older generation who lived under this God's constant scrutiny and were reassured of his punishment if they disobeyed the rules. This God followed them around like the eyes of a holy picture, watching, waiting to pounce, to punish, to test. God was policeman and teacher; the rules and laws he laid down were to be followed without question, without mistake. Just as in covenant, the consequences were made all too clear.

This God is still familiar to us, a frequent visitor to the readings we use in our Eucharistic liturgies. These Old Testament passages, often proclaimed without context or explanation, serve to reinforce our lingering sense of God as an angry, vengeful God who kept score of wrongdoings and who settled scores with those who disappointed or defied him.

> "I mean
> to make her pay!"
> Hosea 1:15a

These messages and images are still in the air around us. We breathe them in almost without noticing. Little wonder that so many good people attend parish retreats expressing complete trust in God's love for them yet still behave as if God was updating their school report and that he had written at the bottom of each daily page in big red letters the words: COULD DO BETTER.

"Where are you?" God asks us and like Adam we reply, "*I was afraid . . . so I hid.*" Little wonder that, in the midst of our whispered fears, we shuffle God and ourselves off into the apparent safety of the good room. There, we use the prayer of polite conversation, with the best of intentions, not realising that it keeps us hidden from sight. We do so because we are afraid; afraid of criticism, punishment and rejection. We handle God like good china; carefully, to avoid breakages.

 ## Show me your face

However much we may be troubled by the pains and poor images of the past, in the very depths of our being we know that we have no reason to hide. We are in the presence of a God who knows our strengths and our weakness, who loves and accepts us and who draws us ever closer

> *Come then, my beloved . . . hiding in the clefts of the rock, in the coverts of the cliff, show me your face .*
> Song of Songs 2: 13, 14

to him. How do we relate to God in a way that allows us to be honest about our fears and concerns? How do we show our faces in our prayer in ways that will foster intimacy and perhaps even help us to have a greater sense of God's nearness to us?

We can only admire how the people of Israel related to the God of the Old Testament. Throughout all the twists and turns of their relationship with him, they experienced God as approachable, even reasonable. Their God was accessible. Their God could receive their joy and praise. He could also receive their fears and their anger. So, if we want a master-class on how to approach God honestly and openly, we need look no further than the example set by Israel's psalmists. Every human emotion, comfortable and uncomfortable finds expression in their verses. They speak as people who are not afraid to show God their faces, to let God know exactly what they are thinking, what they want him to be doing about it, and how annoyed they are when he does not do what he has been asked to do!

One psalm that meets frequently with a resounding 'YES!' when presented in spiritual direction sessions is Psalm 13, already mentioned in Chapter Two above. The psalmist is expressing his anger at God but also is communicating a sense of unwavering trust in God's loving faithfulness. He presents his anger to God, firmly believing that God will not turn him away; God will not reject or abandon him. As we read it below, we might avoid sanitising the gritty sentiment expressed. The psalmist would not have shown polite restraint in delivering these words. He entertained no fear of a God so brittle that he might break under the strain of the anger expressed.

> How long, Yahweh, will you forget me? Forever?
> How long will you turn your face away from me?
> How long must I nurse rebellion in my soul,
> sorrow in my heart day and night?
> How long is the enemy to domineer over me?
> Look down answer me, Yahweh O God!
> Give light to my eyes or I shall fall into the sleep of death.
> Or my foe will boast, 'I have overpowered him,'
> and my enemy have the joy of seeing me stumble.
> As for me, I trust in your faithful love, Yahweh.
> Let my heart delight in your saving help,
> let me sing to Yahweh for his generosity to me,
> let me sing to the name of Yahweh Most High!

This and other psalms allow us to have access and to give expression to the full range of human emotions. Yet it is in the expression of anger that they provide us with a rare gift in our relationship with God. Anger is often an uncomfortable emotion. Experience has taught us that it is not welcome in most relationships. We have been trained to bite our tongue, swallow our anger, stew in our own juices. All of these descriptions suggest some measure of physical pain and hint at the damage that the suppression of anger exerts on the body.

Left unattended, this anger not only damages our health, it affects relationships. It festers inside. Unexpressed anger sits there in the room with us. We can choose to ignore it but we realise, deep down, that things are just not the same. Something is lost in the festering silence; friendships flounder, emotions deaden; love dies.

The same is true of relationship with God. The invitation is to give the anger expression and to trust, just as the psalmists did, that God can take our honesty and concerns, that we have no need to hide. The effects can be quite dramatic. More open with God, we become more aware of God's presence with us in prayer and in daily life. Something in us shifts; we realise that even our most uncomfortable feelings will not cause God to abandon us. We appreciate that God's gift of himself in nearness comes without conditions; his love given freely.

 The hidden God

There are times in our life when the sense of distance we feel between ourselves and God can be alleviated, at least to some degree, by attending to the matters we have discussed above. We risk being ourselves; we flush out of the shadows some of the unhelpful notions we have been entertaining in relation to God. All of this can help us to come to know a God who listens and accepts us, regardless of the mood we bring to him, the dark thoughts we entertain or the mess that surrounds us. We find once again that we are in relationship with a reliable God. The element of security prevails; our familiar prayers and routines retain their capacity to give us comfort and we rest secure in the knowledge that the God on the other side of our words and actions wants to be with us, cares deeply for us.

Security

That said, there are times in our life, perhaps many in number, when, in spite of our honesty and our capacity to be ourselves in prayer, God seems to have abandoned us, or is not behaving in the way we hoped he would. Perhaps we find ourselves facing a family illness or a crisis, a job loss or another major disappointment. Perhaps the past certainties of our faith have come into question and we no longer have easy answers. God does not fit our carefully crafted categories; the old patterns of prayers no longer give comfort, no longer seem to 'work'.

The experience of searching dominates our prayer and it is not the comforting pulse provided by intellectual thirst for more information about God, satisfied by our immersion in clear and well-structured textbooks. Rather it is the aching longing of the psalmist in a desert, without water;[6] lying face down in the dust of his desires. Everything we hold dear - our past security, our belief in God - is shaken to its foundations. We look around at others and assume that they have the kind of faith that we feel ourselves to be lacking. We have lost our certainty and it seems as if we have also lost God. "Why have you forsaken me?" our hearts cry out in the pain of our felt isolation. This experience of the nearness of God feels like the experience of the distance and disappearance of God. Our heads tell us that God is always close but now he feels so very far away.

Searching

Unfortunately, as a Church we lost sight of the fact that God is vast mystery and we have become accustomed to trading in the currency of certainty and security. We have overlooked the uncertainties that pepper centuries of our teaching, and the questions that are so inextricably woven into the fabric of our human existence. Nevertheless, our history is threaded through with a rich seam of searching and struggle, of desert and darkness. Throughout the writings and teachings of the Church, there is a recognition that the God who draws us to himself is a God of mystery, beyond our understanding and words, beyond our certainties and security.

We thus sit in uneasy tension; we have created a climate where faith is synonymous with certainty and yet we know that God remains as unfathomable mystery.[7] In spite of our best efforts and our most comforting certainties, we are forced to concede that we are only scratching the surface of God. We cannot grasp what he is. God remains: *alien to every human eye and hidden from every intellect.*[8.]

Yet, it is in the very desert of God's mystery and of our doubt and darkness that we can stumble upon a new kind of experience of the nearness of God. If we steel ourselves to sit in the dust and to wrap around us the shroud of our past relationship with God, the desert can become the place of encounter with God.[9] He is present there but in ways we can no longer see or feel.

This journey into desert and darkness is a familiar spiritual path.[10] Others, such as John of the Cross[11] and Teresa of Avila have trodden similar paths before us. They know the way. We are invited to trust them and to appreciate that even 'ordinary' people such as us can be called by God into a different experience of his mystery. Teresa and John provide us with sound advice as to how to be with the God who does not seem to be with us.

> *You do very well . . . to seek him as one hidden. You honour God greatly and indeed come near to him, when you hold him to be nobler and deeper than anything you can attain. . . do not be like many heartless people who have a low opinion of God: they think that when they cannot understand him or sense or feel him, he is further away – when the truth is more the opposite: it is when you understand him less clearly that you are coming closer to him*
> John of the Cross

It is in this place of wilderness, of felt-helplessness that we hear the invitation to place ourselves in God's hands and to trust in his loving attentions. Dom Abbot John Chapman describes it in terms of handing ourselves over to the surgeon God. We are asked to place ourselves on the surgeon's table. If we give our YES to the operation, the surgeon with great skill does what he needs to do to heal and restore us. Chapman goes further by asserting that we cannot even help the surgeon by watching him; *'He would act better if you were distracted by something else.'* [12]

In the felt-absence of God, in the darkness, we are asked to trust that even if we do not see or understand what God is doing, we are in good hands. God is working within us; we are being held in his love, even though it does not feel like it. The invitation is to be open with God about the pain of the experience, open about the sense of confusion and bewilderment, the ache of loneliness, the agony of this felt-isolation from him.

> *I thirst for God, the living God, Where shall I go to see the face of God? I have no food but tears day and night, as all day long I am taunted. Where is your God? . . . I shall say to God my rock, 'Why have you forgotten me?'*
> Ps 42: 2,3,9

During such times of darkness – and there can be many - we are asked to trust, and to hear again the words that are so often repeated in scripture, and with good reason: *"Do not be afraid. I am with you."* The invitation is to let yourself be carried by God.[13] This is not an easy task, especially if we have been let down by others in the past. So much more seems to be at stake now. At such times, we will need to rely heavily on what we know of God's faithfulness to his beloved people.

However, at such times it is also unlikely that our prayer will give us much comfort. We are invited to see clues to God's nearness in the events of our lives, in the fruits of his Spirit, in the gestures of love of his people. *"I will be with you always"* this God says to us, the words made flesh, not in our prayer experience but in the people and in the world around us. We are asked to believe that God speaks into the world for us to hear; that his felt absence in prayer is an experience of his nearness; that he is there for us; he would not leave us on our own.[14]

As we noted above, it may seem a self-defeating exercise to bring this work somewhere near its conclusion by dwelling on the painful experience of God's apparent absence but the experience is more common than we might think. Parish retreats and workshops are filled with people who assume that they are losing their faith because they do not "feel" God to be as close as he once was to them. Worse still, they feel alone with their aloneness because everyone else seems to have unlimited access to the Almighty, or so it seems.

We are never alone; God is always with us. We are invited to trust the faithfulness of his commitment to us. We are asked to trust that it is safe to bring ourselves as we really are before the God who loves us. We are asked to believe that we are entrusting ourselves day by day, YES by YES, to a God whose purposeful and transforming nearness is creating in us something new, something unprecedented, a mystery so vast that only God can realise it in us.[15] We are asked to respond in self-giving love to the God who gives himself in love to us. Come! Show your face to the God who aches with love of you, who longs for nearness with you. Come!

FOR YOUR PRAYER AND REFLECTION

SUGGESTION ONE: In the kitchen with Jesus

You probably already have ongoing conversations with God, with Jesus, over the course of your day. Here is a suggestion based on the "empty chair" counselling technique.

Sit at your kitchen table - or wherever you take a break in the day for a cup of tea or a cold drink. Perhaps place a mug or glass at the table and place another empty seat within sight. It can help to imagine that Jesus is sitting there. Talk to him. Tell him what your day has been like so far, mention even the apparently trivial events. Know that he cares, that he is listening.

Questions appear frequently in scripture, a sign of God's desire to engage with his people in two-way conversation, a sign also that he wants to hear from them about what they really think and feel. Include some of these questions in your prayer conversation in the kitchen. Give God your answer, knowing that there is no need to censor your response. Ask him the same questions.

Where are you? (Gen 3:9)

What more could I have done that I have not done? (Isaiah 5: 4)

Who do you say that I am? (Mark 8: 29)

What do you want me to do for you? (Mark 10: 51)

Why did you doubt? (Matt 14:31)

Do you love me? (John 21: 17b)

SUGGESTION TWO: With God in the darkness

John of the Cross proves himself a helpful guide at times when God seems to have disappeared completely, and in spite of our openness and honesty. John recommends forgetting any attempt to meditate or reflect when we come to prayer and simply to sit in as much peace and quiet as we can find. It will feel like a waste of time and the inclination is to become unsettled and to flail about in search of God. However, we are asked to trust that God is there even if we do not feel it. We are being asked 'to do nothing gracefully' and to trust that we are being changed simply by spending time in God's company.

Two activities to help sustain us in the felt-inactivity of prayer:

• we look for God in the daily events of our lives: we will see his fruits in the goodness of others and even this small comfort can be a drop of water in a vast desert

• we read to keep our intellects from being entangled in our experience of prayer and generating more anxiety in us. A good book for this place is: *When the Well Runs dry: Prayer beyond the Beginnings* by Thomas H. Green SJ.

I burn the toast. You might question why a reasonably intelligent person of a certain age and a fair amount of experience in the kitchen cannot manage to brown a simple piece of bread to its correct state of 'brownness'. I can offer passable excuses but, deep down, I know the real reason; other distractions seem to provide a much more entertaining use of my time. A quick phone call, a few pages of a book; I will use any excuse to avoid watching toast.

Yet my girls love toast: "Golden brown toast, please mummy," they would say when they were young. Translated, this meant, "Not your sooty black specialty, please." I had choices to make. My children loved toast and I loved my children. Presented with two hungry children, nothing else mattered but providing them with food. So, I set aside something good for something better; my little sacrifice, a reflection of a greater love.

It may seem very frivolous to introduce the subject of burning toast into this final stage of the serious business of our reflection on the nearness of God. However, the topic is pertinent. God's nearness to us has one purpose; to draw us into self-giving union with him, a union which will be lived out in God's dream of Kingdom. In this loving harmony with Father, Son and Holy Spirit and with each other, our existence will be in balance again because God will be at its centre. We will live a GOD-first life; everything else will fall into its right place.

7. KNOWING WHAT MATTERS

RESTING IN THE NEARNESS OF GOD

. . .only one thing is needed. Mary has chosen the better part and it is not to be taken away from her.
Luke 10: 42

However, we know that God will not force his self-giving nearness upon us. Instead, he gives us the freedom to choose relationship with him. His gift of freedom presents us with choices. Do we *want* nearness with God? Do we *want* to know him and for him to know us? Do we *want* a life where God matters so much to us that he is the reason shaping and forming our every choice, our every word and every action.

The idea of choosing nearness with God might seem strange to us when the standard practice of our Church is to baptise infants, in other words, to choose *for* them. Yet nearness *is* a choice and it is a risky choice. It invites us to come out into the open, to be seen by God as we truly are and to be as vulnerable in love with God as he is vulnerable in love with us.

Intimacy with God is a risky business. We are in love with a vast and marvellous mystery. At some level, we need to know that we are safe with this mystery; that God has our best interests at heart. If our lives are to be shaped around him and centred on him, we need not only to be told that God cares about us but also we need to know for ourselves that we are loved by him. We need to know in our hearts that we matter to God.

In this book, we have been reminded that God's nearness is creative and purposeful; his presence with and within us gives us everything we need to live and grow in his love. In these closing pages, we could bring our search to its conclusion, as other books do, with a summary and analysis of the material above and a few suggestions for action. God's nearness is transforming us; we are becoming his nearness in the world. What does this mean for us? What do we do about it? The questions are useful but to address them too soon may be to create the impression that God's nearness is insistently purposeful; that we are loved because we serve God's purpose, rather than loved simply because we exist, and that we exist because we are loved![1]

Attention to such questions might also unnecessarily rush the movement from reflection to activity. Remember Martha and Mary in Luke's gospel. Luke was using their story as a counterweight to the preceding missionary activity of the seventy-two disciples (Luke 10). Luke's implicit message was that all activity must be rooted in relationship, nurtured by time spent with Jesus. We need that time with God. We need to linger at his feet not only because we need to know and love him but also because, in his presence, we will come to know just how much we are loved by him; day by day, we will come to know that we matter to God.

So here in this book, we heed Luke's advice and linger with the Lord. We do this by savouring a few of the experiences of nearness we have touched on above. In this chapter, we will spend time with God – Father, Son or Spirit - being ourselves, basking in God's nearness in whatever way it makes itself available to us.

This is not to be viewed as an escape from the challenges of, and the need for, activity. We cannot reflect on the material in this book without feeling some sense of pain at the existing gaps in Church and in ourselves, or without seeing the challenge presented to each one personally to recognise and fulfil his or her role in bringing about God's dream. These tensions and others are within us now. However, we choose not to rattle about in the kitchen of these particular concerns for the moment. Instead, we will linger with God by reflecting on three different passages of scripture. Each is selected to enable us to be with different dimensions of the experience of God's nearness, to encourage our own sense of nearness to God and our own awareness that we matter to him.

Ever at play in his presence

We begin with a passage from the book of Proverbs that presents God's wisdom as another person. As Christians, we can see in this passage a glimpse of the person to come: Christ.[2] As we share in Christ's relationship with the Father, it is not unreasonable for us to insert ourselves into this passage and to claim the experience as our own. In the words which follow, we encounter a God who has loved each one of us from eternity and are asked to believe that there was never a moment that our lives and our destinies were not embraced by his love.[3] This passage puts words and images on the joyful reality of God's love for each one of us, his delight in us.

> *The Wisdom of God cries aloud:*
> *The Lord created me when his purpose first*
> *unfolded, before the oldest of his works. From*
> *everlasting, I was firmly set, from the beginning,*
> *before the earth came into being . . .when he fixed*
> *the heavens firm, I was there . . . when he laid down*
> *the foundations of the earth, I was by his side, a*
> *master-craftsman, delighting him day after day, ever*
> *at play in his presence, at play everywhere in his*
> *world, delighting to be with the sons of men.*
> Proverbs 8: 22-31

This is such a beautiful passage of freedom and joy and delight. How often we associate God with duty and responsibility and, assume that surrendering ourselves to nearness with him equates to volunteering for a spiritual obstacle race of suffering and sorrow. Life is tough and we cannot deny the suffering that happens as a natural consequence of frail bodies and selfish desires for wealth and power. We cannot deny the presence of suffering in our world However, this scripture is an invitation to savour a dimension of God's nearness that is so often overlooked; the nearness of a God who created us for joy; who created us for play: a God who invites us to have life and to have it to the full (John 10:10).

How, in the sober and serious circumstances of our adult lives, buckling under the weight of countless responsibilities, do we help ourselves to get in touch with that place in us where we are still at play with God, that deep centre of our being where God delights in us, and where we delight in him? We do not connect with that place by running away from our troubles. We know our burdens; God sees them, too, and knows our struggle with them, However, we realise that there is another place in us where God is in nearness with us also; a place of joy. We have simply forgotten where it is.

The child in us remembers. That place in us where we keep the good memories from childhood is still there. It is a place of fun; a place accessible to us in our recall of the rocks we scampered over with grazed knees, the leaves we threw about, the puddles we splashed in, the streets where we played. The child in us remembers how to have fun. By revisiting our childhood memories, we might reacquaint ourselves with that child so that our adult selves can remember what it is to wake with delight into a new day, a day stretching ahead with all its promise.

If our childhood was not an experience of freedom and fun, we can as adults try to create that playful space within us by using our imagination. We can call to mind our favourite place, somewhere we feel free and at home. It could be a hillside where we can 'get above it all'; or on a bike, sailing down the road, wind on face, road stretching ahead of us . . . or on a beach . . . or on a park bench . . . or . . . the possibilities are endless. In our imaginations, we can go to places where our bodies in real life may no longer be able to take us. Wherever we choose, we are free in that place for now, free from the worries of the world; free to be; to enjoy this moment.

 That feeling of joy and freedom is the 'backing track' to this piece of scripture. It weaves its way throughout, playing its joyful melody as the images unfold. Before reading it again, think also of this. Each morning, even after eighteen years, I rouse my children from their sleep and I feel as if it is my birthday and I am opening my presents again. It gives me a glimpse of God's excitement. We are beautifully wrapped presents, to be opened by a grateful God who delights in our presence, who is excited to be with us, who waits for us to wake each morning so that he can spend the day with us. In his infinite love for us, God never loses that sense of expectation and of joy at what is being unwrapped before him, created within us with his loving help.

Can we imagine God with us in our place of freedom and joy? Can we hear again his invitation to play, so that we might enjoy and *for this moment* delight in his company, trusting that he delights in ours? God created us for love and laughter; he cares about each one of us and has done so since the beginning of time. Each one of us created so that Love might give himself to us; born for nearness; you and I; the reason for God's delight. Can we believe it?

143

Lord
To find a part of me where joy resides;
Where each new day is unwrapped gift from you;
Where I know myself as I truly am:
The source of your delight;
Beloved child.
Creator God,
Excited God,
Delighted God,
Teach me to play.

With you

We leave this scene of playfulness and freedom behind, knowing that we can return to it whenever we wish: we carry this place somewhere within us. We move on to our second reflection, which centres on the raising of Lazarus (John 11: 1-44). However, we adopt something of a playful approach here, presenting a very different version of events to those given by John. The aim of our mischief is to explore what will prove to be a serious dimension of our experience of the nearness of God.

We might imagine Lazarus, a middle-aged Jewish tradesman - a weaver or a basket maker. Let us imagine also that he has two teenage sons who are searching for their own trades, and three daughters who each need a good husband and a decent dowry. Lazarus, his wife, five children and the wife's mother all live together in their tiny house. Lazarus is forced to work long hours so that he might provide for his family. Providing enough food and clothing is proving to be more and more of a struggle; what little sleep he gets is troubled and fitful.

Lazarus's life is an endless cycle of working, eating, sleeping, with no prospect of change. It does change one day, however, when Lazarus collapses; his forehead blazing like a furnace, a sharp pain piercing his stomach. Fevered days follow sleepless nights; cold cloths are placed on his body but to no avail. The women of the house surround him; seated, they sing their songs of mourning. But the songs and the sounds of crying grow dimmer with each passing day until Lazarus finds himself shrouded by only silence and darkness; plunged into the sleep of the dead.

It is so still and cool and quiet in the tomb where they have laid him to rest. Lazarus is aware of nothing until a familiar voice penetrates the darkness, calling his name: *"Lazarus, come out."* Lazarus, tied hand and foot with burial bands, slowly opens his eyes, breathes deeply his first new breath, inhaling the blackness of the cave around him. He moves further into the tomb's comforting stillness, wrapping himself in this new cloak of shadowy silence, and he whispers, "You must be joking!"

> *He cried out in a loud voice, "Lazarus, come out!" (John 11: 43)*

A comment before we move into reflection on the story itself. In this book, we have not attended to the spectacular, the miraculous, or to the personal visions that can also be part of the experience of God's nearness in the world. The omission is deliberate. The inclusion of references to such occurrences would have required detailed and specific attention to the discernment of the validity of such, and this is given more thorough attention in other texts.[4] Moreover, their inclusion would have blurred one of the key purposes of this work, namely, to explore a central and recurring fact apparent in God's dealings with our humanity: that God does his most spectacular work in ordinary people; that each one of us is a spectacular work of God.

For this reason, when we reflect on this story of Lazarus, we are not going to be focussing on the miracle of Lazarus's resurrection. Instead, in our friend Lazarus we are to recognise a man carrying the burdens of an ordinary life; a man not marvelling at miracles but stuck in the darkness, reluctant to come out. This is a less pleasant place to explore than the place of play and joy visited above. However, our visit to the tomb will prove fruitful; it will help us to identify another dimension of the experience of the nearness of God.

To locate ourselves in the tomb with poor Lazarus, we need first to remember what we might refer to as 'duvet days'. These are days when we feel the need to hide away in bed, safely entombed in quilted comfort, buried until the chaos inside abates, tiredness leaves us and we have energy again to face the world. We recognise the bed as a soft and temporary tomb. However, when duvet days give way to months of tiredness, when trapped by illness, pain or difficult circumstances, we can feel ourselves caught within the solid and more sinister walls of a different tomb. Where is God now?

It is reasonable to think of the tomb as we would of Elijah's cave (1 Kings 19: 9-18). Elijah is in hiding from those, including Queen Jezebel, who would wish to see him dead. In this scripture, we read that the Lord is gently calling him out of the cave and into the open. God is calling him out to face the difficulties and challenges of his life, promising help for what lies ahead. The same God offers assistance and energy to us so that we might face the challenges that life brings, trusting in his nearness with us.

However, the experience of the tomb is not always as a place from which one must escape in order to be with God. Quite often, it is a very difficult if not impossible place to leave; painful emotions sap our energy; fear or anger has us in its grip; illness or circumstances render us with feelings of genuine helplessness.

146

We might choose to ignore the tiredness, or struggle with illness in the hope that it will go away. We might try to plan and pare our lives, to rein in or remove uncomfortable or unwanted emotions, reschedule and reorganise our busy days and make ourselves into 'better' people.  Yet experience would suggest that many such efforts effect only temporary relief. Sooner or later, the tomb calls us back and we find ourselves sitting once again in the dark.

The thing now is not to fight the darkness, nor to organise our lives to ignore the black walls around us, or the sense of emptiness we might feel. We have before us a surprising invitation - to see the tomb, and the darkness, as did the Celts and the mystics of old;[5] to see darkness as a place of growth. Furthermore, and most importantly, we are asked trust that God is present with us there. He did not create this darkness but neither is he going to abandon us to it. God will not leave us on our own.

The inclination remains to devise an escape, and to involve God in such, by praying for the things we think we need in order to get out. Nevertheless, the invitation of the dark is to explore the dark, to claim for ourselves what it feels like to be in this tomb and then to bring our tomb experience – and not our escape plan – to God in prayer.[6] The questions change, they centre now on actual experience and the real 'you' who comes before God. What is it like to feel stuck? What is it like to feel alone, to know that in spite of our best efforts nothing seems to change? How do we feel about ourselves in this place? A failure? A mess? Afraid? Angry? Where is God ?

Our *lived* experience of the tomb now becomes the substance of the conversation with God and we can find ourselves in the presence of the God who *sees* and understands, the God who knows and loves us. "It's all right," he says, not belittling our experience but, instead, acknowledging our struggle in it all. Then, we know that there is no need to pretend with him; we are loved in spite of the mess that seems to litter our lives; we know that we matter to God.

In this way, the tomb becomes a place of growth in darkness. *The place where you are standing **is** holy ground* (Exodus 3: 5) because it is a place of the raw encounter with God. We would not invite such an experience, we do not earn or deserve it, nor would God deliberately locate us in any place of pain; but we are here and he is with us. The God-man, Jesus, suffered death, entered his own tomb rather than deny God's love or abandon his people. His love is strong as death; stronger than any darkness in any tomb; overwhelming, relentless, unstoppable..

Whatever tomb we may find ourselves in now or in the future, we can trust that we are not alone in there; God would not leave us on our own; he is there with us. "*Lazarus, come out,*" Jesus says in the gospel. In our version of events, the same Jesus adds: "And if you don't, I'll come in and sit with you . . . for as long as you need.' He meant it when he said, "*I will be with you always*" (Matt 28: 20).

Lord
when shadows of my sad self block out
your light
when I hide from life
too hard to live
when pain has me in its grip
and tears are all I have
to quench my thirst;
let me cry with you
and know that
in the darkness
you are crying too.
With me.

Beloved child

In this final reflection, we exchange the darkness for the mountain mist and follow Jesus and his disciples up a high mountain to witness his transfiguration (Matt 17: 1-8). The story is rich in symbolism, suggesting that it is a theological rather than a historical account.[7] Nevertheless, we can be sure that those disciples saw a transformation in Jesus so exquisitely beautiful that words alone were not enough to capture the power and the significance of what unfolded before them.[8]

To locate ourselves in this scene, we might remember a place where that intense moment of awareness of God's presence in our lives takes hold of us, snatching us out of ourselves, as if on a roller-coaster ride, carrying us in an instant to heights and depths that are both exhilarating and frightening. One such place for me is on the cliff edge of the Antrim plateau as it drops abruptly to the sea near the Giants Causeway. Standing close to the edge on a summer's day is an experience of breathtaking, jaw-dropping beauty. Blue sky stretches seamlessly over land and sea; the strata of the exposed cliff face lying like leather-bound books piled clumsily one atop the other, the land buckled and broken by hundreds and thousands of years of heart-stopping, mind-blowing movement and change.

To stand at this place on the cliff-edge, precariously poised within sight of the dangerous waves pummelling the rocks below, is to feel oneself to be in that place which connects life and death, now and eternity. And it is to encounter a God who is greater than the force of waves, greater than the slow grinding earth, twisting layers of rock like pages of a book; greater than the hundreds and thousands of years which brought this life and this land to this place. It is to encounter the same God the disciples met on that mountaintop on that day.

Six days later, Jesus took with him Peter and James and his brother John and led them up a high mountain by themselves. There in their presence he was transfigured: his face shone like the sun and his clothes became as dazzling as light. And suddenly Moses and Elijah appeared to them; they were talking with him. Then Peter spoke to Jesus. "Lord," he said, "it is wonderful for us to be here; if you want me to I will make three shelters, one for you, one for Moses and one for Elijah." He was still speaking when suddenly a bright cloud covered them with shadow and from the cloud there came a voice which said, "This is my Son the beloved; he enjoys my favour. Listen to him." When they heard this, the disciples fell on their faces, overcome with fear. But Jesus came up and touched them, saying, "Stand up, do not be afraid." And when they raised their eyes they saw no one but Jesus. (Matt 17: 1-8)

The sense of the amazing power and majesty of God is at the heart of the disciples' experience of transfiguration. God was present to them that day in all his breathtaking, jaw-dropping, heart-stopping, mind-blowing glory. It was an experience beyond their wildest imaginings and beyond their words, and they relied on symbols to communicate their awareness of God's nearness on that mountain. [9]

In our twenty-first century seats, we connect with the mystery by connecting with our own place of breath-taking wonder and read the passage again knowing that we do so in the presence of the Risen Christ. What was happening then is happening again now. It will also help us to understand the gospel as the early followers did, recognising the images used are as scriptural sound bites, single words conveying centuries of understanding of God's love for his people.

The location of the transfiguration is itself significant. A mountain is a symbolic holy place, a place where God is known to be at work. The image conveys a sense of the air tingling with anticipation at what God is about to do, the vastness of the landscape a reflection of his vast and mighty mystery. God's presence is revealed in all its beauty and glory not just in the scene and setting but also in the face of Christ radiant like the sun, revealing God's glory (2 Cor 4: 6). God is powerfully at work in this place.

The images used invite us to be aware of God's presence in another way. Moses and Elijah appear to remind us of God's gift of himself in his Word and in his Law.[10] Creation looks on in wonder as all of God's promises, his love and longing converge on a single point: Christ, God's fullest and finest declaration of faithfulness to his people. God's Word is made flesh in Jesus, his Law fulfilled in this ultimate gesture of love.[11] He is here!

God's mystery and majesty envelops the scene. We see God, descending symbolically, in the form of cloud.[12] A voice reaches through this cloud from its place in eternity and God shouts his love for the beloved who stands before him. He is here! Transfiguration, transformation unfolds. Nothing will ever be the same again.

He is here! God's transforming nearness, his glory and greatness made visible in the person of Christ. It is a story of another transformation, a transformation of breath-taking beauty. It is a story of our transformation in baptism.[13] Here, the holy place of encounter between ourselves and God is not the mountain but a place deep within, where his Spirit dwells (1 Cor 3: 16). In this encounter, God is powerfully at work, offering himself to us anew; offering us a share in his life of love.

We are changed; what happens so visibly in Jesus happens in us in places we do not see. Soaked in God's Spirit-Water, bathing in God's light we become *pneuma*, a new creation; we become like Christ. In baptism, all of God's love and longing converge on a single point. The new believer is invited into new life, the symbols making visible the mystery of God's transforming presence and action. We find ourselves once again surrounded by the mystery and majesty of God, find ourselves in that place between death and life, between NOW and eternity. We hear, in some place deep within God shouting aloud as he did on that mountain his love for his beloved child.

Such is the jaw-dropping, mind-blowing, breath-taking, heart-stopping encounter with God in baptism. It is the God who lives in self-giving nearness within each one of us; the God who, day after day, reaches across his eternity to us, offering us, each day anew, the chance to share with him his life of love. His nearness to us changes us. Transformation unfolds. Nothing will ever be the same again.

*. . . reflecting
the glory of God . . .
being transformed into
the image that we reflect
in brighter and brighter
glory . . .*
2 Cor 3: 18

*Lord,
You gave me life;
Loved me into being.
I give my life to you
That I may live
In love
With you.
God of high mountains
and holy places:
Breath-taking God,
Mind-blowing God,
Transforming God.
Fill me:
With you.*

If only we knew what God was offering . . . The final reflection on the transfiguration account emphasises the value of symbols in communicating what words alone fail to capture. We will never be able to grasp the full height, depth and breadth of the experience of nearness on offer from God. The God who created us for love, who pledged himself in love to us and who gave himself in love for us, again and again, is beyond words; his love beyond our wildest imaginings; his desire for nearness with us beyond our craziest dreams.

 We have tried in this book to catch something of the experience of God's nearness through words and images; the resurrection plant, the love of a mother for her child, the pledge of commitment communicated in covenant, the shepherd king, the Spirit breath, the lover God, the Body of Christ. All are but a glimpse, a small taste, of the vast banquet on offer from God himself. Eventually, we are forced to sit in wordless wonder, to sit in awe of the amazing love of a God who wants a relationship of nearness with us.

In bringing our journey to a close, I will avoid the pitfalls of summing up the self-giving, creative and purposeful nearness of God. There are no sound-bites, no pithy punch-lines that could ever hope to capture the ongoing and eternal thirst of God for nearness with us. Instead, in parting, I leave the final word to God himself as we reflect together on a few of God's words of love gathered from scripture. These words are now focussed on you; written that you might believe that God wants nearness with you, that you might truly and deeply believe that you matter to him. They are words of love to be carried by you to others as you continue to experience and *to be* an experience of the nearness of God in the world.

And now, God speaks to you

He who created you

Do not be afraid for I bring you new life   *Isaiah 43: 1*

I have known your name before you were born

And now, I use that name to call you

I was the one who formed you with love   *Psalm 139:13, 14*

in your mother's womb

And with love gave you life

My beloved child, you are a wonder!

You are so precious to me;

I love you with a love that will never die.   *Isaiah 43: 19*

I am building a new life for us, a new heaven   *Isaiah 54: 10*

where we can live in loving nearness together

And I have already begun this new life together

in you, my new creation   *2 Cor 5:17*

Do not be afraid   *Mark6:50*

Believe in me; trust in me   *John 12:44*

Live in me; as I live in you   *John 14: 1*

Trust that I have lived and died for you   *John17:21*

That I gave my life in love of you   *John 15:13*

That nothing will separate you from my love.   *Romans 8: 38, 39*

And that I will be with you. Always.   *Matt 28: 20*

SUGGESTIONS FOR FURTHER READING

1. From the Beginning
Joseph Ratzinger, *In the Beginning* (Burn & Oates: New York, 2005).
Christopher West, *Theology of the Body Explained: A Commentary on John Paul II's Gospel of the Body* (Gracewing: Leominster, 2003).

2. Led by Love
Walter Brueggemann, *An Unsettling God* (Fortress Press: Minneapolis, 2009).

3. Love is Strong as death
Enda Lyons, *Jesus: Self Portrait by God* (Columba Press: Dublin, 1994).
Gerald O'Collins SJ, *Jesus: Our Redeemer* (Oxford University Press, 2007)

4. Becoming what you receive
Kenan Osborne, *Community Eucharist and Spirituality* (Liguori: Missouri, 2007).

5. Come!
William Bausch SJ, *A New Look at Sacraments* (Twenty-third Publications: New York, 1983).
Joseph Martos, *Doors to the Sacred: A Historical Introduction to Sacraments in the Catholic Church* (Liguori: Missouri, updated and revised edition, 2001).

6. Where are you?
Thomas Green SJ, *When the Well Runs dry: Prayer Beyond the Beginnings (Ave Maria Press: Notre Dame, 1979)*.
Iain Matthew, *The Impact of God (Hodder & Stoughton: London,1995)*.

7. Knowing what matters:
Martin Laird, *Into the Silent Land: The Practice of Contemplation* (Darton, Longman & Todd: London, 2006).
Gerard Hughes, *God of Surprises* (Darton, Longman & Todd: London, 1985).

CHAPTER NOTES

Abbreviations used

Vat II	Documents of Vatican II
GS	Gaudium et spes
LG	Lumen gentium
AG	Ad gentes

Jerome	The Jerome Biblical Commentary Eds. R.E. Brown, J.A. Fitzmeyer, R.E. Murphy, (Geoffrey Chapman: London, reprint 1977) Volume 1 or 2 stated, followed by chapter number and number of paragraph. For example, Vol 2 77:46 is Volume 2, chapter 77, paragraph number 46.

INTRODUCTION: A WORLD FULL OF GOD

[1] Gerard Manley Hopkins SJ, 'My Own Heart' in *A Choice of Poets* *(Harrap: London, 1968)* 118.

[2] Blessed Angela Foligno, quoted in Pierre Tielhard de Chardin, *Le Milieu Divin: An essay on the Interior Life* (Collins: London, 1960) 104.

[3] Karl Rahner SJ, Theological Investigations, Volume 5 (CD compiled by the Centre of Culture, Technology and Values, Mary Immaculate College, Limerick, Ireland.) 3.

[4] St Augustine, *The Confessions of St Augustine*, Book 1, page 1.

[5] Martin Luther, *Disputations against Scholastic Theology* quoted in Oswald Bayer, *Theology the Lutheran Way*, Ed and Trans.: Jeffrey G. Silcock, Mark C. Mattes (W.B. Eermans Pub Co: Michigan, 2007) 274.

CHAPTER ONE: FROM THE BEGINNING

[1] Compare this with *'My love is mine and I am his'*, Song of Songs 2: 16.

[2] Karl Rahner SJ, *Theological Investigations* V 1 (page 211 on CD version; The Way) 311. Also: CCC #356.

[3] CCC #341.

[4] Genesis is an amalgamation of texts of various ages, written between the 10th and the 5th Centuries BC. Jerome 1; 1: 13.

[5] CCC #283.

[6] CCC#337; CCC #289.

[7] The Hebrew word *ruach* has several meanings: air, spirit, wind and holy breath. This interplay between wind, spirit and breath also applies to ruach's equivalent in Greek (*pneuma*) and Latin (*spiritus*). Ignace de la Potterie SJ, *The Hour of Jesus* (St Paul Publications: Slough 1989) 163.

[8] Joseph Ratzinger, *In the beginning* (Burn & Oates: New York, 2005) 64-5.

[9] Ratzinger, *In the beginning*, 64-5.

[10] CCC #49 quoting *GS #3*.

[11] *Jerome1*; 2:6.

[12] Joseph Ratzinger, 'The New Covenant: A theology of covenant in the New Testament' in *Communio*, 1995(4), 635-651, 651.

[13] The Hebrew writers of Genesis had no concept of or word for soul. It is unlikely that this passage points to God's creation of the human soul as some have concluded in the past. Walter Brueggemann, *An Unsettling God* (Fortress Press: Minneapolis, 2009) 60.

[14] *'Adam . . . prefigured the One who was to come'* (Romans 5:14).

[15] John Paul II, *Theology of Body* (Pauline Books and Media: Slough, 1997) 51ff.

[16] John Paul II, *Theology of Body* 51ff.

[17] Ratzinger, *In the beginning*, 65.

[18] Joseph Ratzinger, New Covenant, 635.

[19] CCC # 1730 quoting *GS #17*.

[20] CCC #400 .

[21] Ratzinger, *In the Beginning*, 72.

[22] This takes us into the territory of 'original sin' but there term is deliberately omitted from this work because the term is open to

misunderstanding (See Ratzinger, In the Beginning, 72.) For a good introduction to the practice of infant baptism and the related teaching, see: William Bausch SJ, *A New Look at Sacraments* (Twenty-third Publications: New London, 1983) 65-77. Baptism is also considered further in chapters below.

[23] Ratzinger, *In the Beginning*, 72. Ratzinger is staying close to the understanding of orginal sin and is pointing to it as an inner tendency and not the result of the impact of one's environment. He recognizes humanity's inner proclivity for broken relationships with self, others and God. See also GS #13.

[24] John Paul II reminds us that the love God gave to man in creation was given irrevocably: *Theology of the Body*, 167. See also CCC #705

[25] John Paul II refers to the 'unrepeatability' of the human person in *Theology of the Body*, 78.

[26] Karl Rahner SJ, *Meditations on the Sacraments* (Burns and Oates: London, 1977) 2-3.

[27] Tertullian (2nd / Early 3rd Century), quoted in Gerald O'Collins, *Jesus: Our Redeemer* (Oxford University Press, 2007) 37. See also: Benedict XVI, "Adam and Christ: from original sin to freedom."Sermon December 3, 2008.

[28] CCC #705.

CHAPTER TWO: LED BY LOVE

[1] *Jerome* Vol 2; 77: 74-98.

[2] *Jerome* Vol 1; 3:44.

[3] Steven L. McKenzie, *Covenant* (Chalice Press: St Louis, 2000) 1-10.

[4] Examples of such covenants are found in scripture: Joshua 9: 11-5, 1 Samuel 11:1. *Dictionary of Biblical theology* Ed: Xavier Leon-Dufour (Geoffrey Chapman: London, 1995) 93.

[5] *Jerome*, Vol 1; 3: 44.

[6] *Jerome, Vol 2*; 77: 77-80.

[7] McKenzie, *Covenant*, 18.

[8] The expression 'cutting a covenant' stemmed from this movement between the halved or 'cut' animals.

[9] Jerome Vol 1; 4:36.

[10] *Jerome Vol 1*, 77: 68.

[11] McKenzie, *Covenant*, 141.

[12] Walter Brueggemann, *Out of Babylon* (Abington Press: Nashville, 2010) 3

[13] Brueggemann, *Unsettling God*, 23.

[14] Inclusion of covenant in Abram's story is a historical anachronism. Covenant did not enter Israel's experience until many centuries after Abraham. However, its use here is not an accident. As already mentioned, Israel saw covenant as a way defining her relationship with God . It seemed fitting to assume that covenant was part of her story and from the beginning. McKenzie, *Covenant* 16; Brueggemann, *Unsettling God* 24.

[15] Brueggemann, *Unsettling God*, 21.

[16] McKenzie, *Covenant*, 17.

[17] *Jerome* 1; 3:8.

[18] Brueggemann, *Unsettling God*, 26.

[19] Brueggemann, *Unsettling God* 24.

[20] The stipulations were presented in the Book of Exodus (20: 1-17) and as Law codes in the Book of Deuteronomy (Chapters 12-26). See Steven McKenzie *Covenant*, 37.

[21] See Timothy Radcliffe OP., *What is the point of being a Christian?* (Burns and Oates: London, 2005) 43. Radcliffe quote in this paragraph taken from same source.

[22] *Jerome* Vol 1; 3:67

[23] *Jerome Vol 1*, Chapter 77: par. 68

[24] Brueggemann, *An Unsettling God*, 22.

[25] Brueggemann, *An Unsettling God*, 25.

[26] *Jerome*, Vol 2; 77: 100.

[27] Brueggemann, *An Unsettling God*, 4. See also CCC #370 *In no way is God in man's image . . .*

[28] Brueggemann, *An Unsettling God*, 4.

[29] *Dictionary of Biblical Theology*, Leon-Dufour, 541

[30] *Jerome*, Vol 2; 42:39.

[31] 2 Sam 7: 12-14.

[32] CCC #2779; CCC #42.

[33] Brueggemann, 39. *An Unsettling God*

[34] Brueggemann, *An Unsettling God* 40; CCC #2589.
[35] Brueggemann, *An Unsettling God*, 40.
[36] Brueggemann, *An Unsettling God*, 22; CCC #2560.

CHAPTER THREE: LOVE AS STRONG AS DEATH

[1] Sam Mc Bratney, *Guess how much I love you* (Walker Books Ltd: London, 1994).
[2] Enda Lyons, *Jesus: Self Portrait by God* (Columba Press: Dublin, 1994).
[3] *Song of Songs* 8:6 The Collegeville Bible Commentary,Gen Eds Diane Bergant C.S.A. & Robert J. Karris, O.F.M. (The Liturgical Press: Minnesota,1998) 796.
[4] Bernard McGinn, *The Foundations of Mysticism* (Crossroad: New York, 1986) 86.
[5] *Jerome* Vol. II 77: 52-163.
[6] Jerome Vol I 22: 48.
[7] Way of prayer is quoted and elaborated upon in Anthony de Mello, *Sadhana: A Way to God* (Doubleday New York, 1978) 119-10
[8] Ian Matthew *The Impact of God*: *Soundings from St John of the Cross* (Hodder & Stoughton: London, 1995) 112.
[9] Laurence Jaffe, *Liberating the Heart: Spirituality and Jungian Psychology* (Inner City Books: Toronto, 1990) 84.
[10] William A. Barry, William J. Connolly, *The Practice of Spiritual Direction* (HarperSan Francisco, 1982) 86.
[11] Hans Urs von Balthasar SJ, *Prayer* (Ignatius Press: San Francisco, 1986) Piece in call out box is from p95.
[12] Gerard O'Collins offers this and more extensive definitions of salvation and redemption in his book *Jesus: Our Redeemer* (Oxford University Press, 2007) 3-18.
[13] Dermot Lane, *The Reality of Jesus* (Paulist Press: New York, 1975) 41.
[14] Lane, *The Reality of Jesus*, 41.
[15] Did God will Jesus' death? This is too big a subject to handle here but it is addressed by O'Collins in *Jesus Our Redeemer*, quoted above. His central point is communicated in the following: *'the self-sacrificing death of Jesus was not due to his positive and direct will (nor that of the Father) but to the abuse of human freedom on the part of the religious*

and political leaders whose vested interests were threatened by the uncompromising message of Jesus. (p171).

[16] *Jerome* Vol 2; 44: 156. See reference to blood ties in Chapter Two above. Christ as New Covenant; CCC #612-614.

[17] GS #22.

[18] CCC # 460.

CHAPTER FOUR: BECOMING WHAT YOU RECEIVE

[1] Susan Varley, *Badger's Parting Gifts* (Collins: London, 2002).

[2] We remember that there are two accounts of Pentecost. The account in John is different from that laid down in Acts. The early Church accepted both accounts, both taken to be describing the coming of the same Spirit. *The Gospel according to John XIII-XXI*, The Anchor Bible, Translation and notes by Raymond Brown (Geoffrey Chapman: London, 1972) 1036-1039.

[3] *Jerome* Vol II 63: 177.

[4] CCC#727.

[5] Some theologians argue that God does not dwell within the individual until that person says YES to God's offer of relationships. Others assumed that the YES would also have required that the individual's soul were pure enough to receive such a divine guest. In this book we favour the position held by theologians such as Karl Rahner: that God indwells within our humanity at all times; that he is present as an offer of relationship. We do not need to tidy the house in preparation for him. God is already there and with our cooperation will provide everything we need and from within to help us to make a positive response to his invitation to relationship. Karl Rahner, *Foundations of Christian Faith: An introduction to the idea of Christianity*, Trans William V. Dych (Darton, Longman and Todd: London, 1978) 121-133.

[6] CCC # 606. Irenaeus (in call-out box) quoted in Raniero Cantalamessa SJ, *Life in the Lordship of Christ: A Spiritual Commentary on the Letter to the Romans*, (Sheed & Ward: London, 1990) 224.

[7] Rahner, *Foundations* 139.

[8] *Collegeville Bible Commentary*, 1007.

[9] CCC #737.

[10] Bernard McGinn, *The Foundations of Mysticism*, 86.

[11] Paul's criterion for evaluating all gifts is that they are given for the good of the community. See: *Collegeville Bible Commentary*, 1127.

[12] CCC #788, Vat II *Lumen Gentium #7*.

[13] *Jerome*, 56:30.

[14] For a concise summary of the early practices and beliefs see Joseph Martos, *Doors to the Sacred: A Historical Introduction to Sacraments in the Catholic Church* (Liguori: Missouri, 2001) 214 -218.

[15] McGinn, *The Foundations of Mysticism*, 86.

[16] Kenan Osborne, *Community Eucharist and Spirituality* (Liguori: Missouri, 2007) 20 -21.

[17] Martos, *Doors to the Sacred*,*216-217*

[18] Osborne, *Community, Eucharist, Spirituality*, 29.

[19] See Martos, *Doors to the Sacred* for a development of the history of Eucharist; 209-274.

[20] Vat II, *Sacrosanctum concilium* #14; CCC #1141.

[21]Osborne, *Community, Eucharist and Spirituality*, Chapter one. Osborne highlights the fundamental importance of the existence of a thriving 'Jesus community' as the basis for the celebration of Eucharist.

[22] CCC # 1088

[23] CCC #1362.

[24]*Joseph Ratzinger, God is Near Us: The Eucharist, the Heart of Life.* (Ignatius Press: San Francisco, 2001) 86.

[25] Augustine *Confessions* Book 7,10:16

CHAPTER FIVE: COME!

[1] Raymond E. Brown, *The Community of the Beloved Disciple : The life, loves and hates of an Individual Church in New Testament times* (Paulist Press: New York, 1979) 40-43.

[2] From Bartimaeus story, Mark 10:49 - 54

[3] Martos, *Doors to the Sacred, 148-153*

[4] Based on Acts 19 and information presented by Maxwell E. Johnston, *The Rites of Initiation; the evolution and interpretation* (Litugical Press: Minnesota, 2007) and Martos, *Doors to the Sacred* Chapter 6.

[5] Johnston, *Rites of Initiation*, 23 – 37; Martos, *Doors to the Sacred*, 148.

[6] Martos, *Doors to the Sacred*, 27.

[7] "mysteries" in Jerusalem Bible is rendered by the phrase "*secret acts of God*" in Christian community bible, Catholic Pastoral edition.

[8] 29. Tertullian 210AD. Martos, *Doors to the Sacred*, 25, 28, 29

[9] St Leo the Great, quoted in CCC #1115. We can we say that the sacraments were "instituted" by Christ, not because he sat down with his disciples and gave instructions as to how they would carry out certain and specific rites but because the sacraments represent a continuation of and participation in the saving work Jesus initiated while on earth. See also CCC #1113 and 1114.

[10] A good account of the evolution of the 'Rites of Initiation' can be found in Martos, *Doors to the Sacred*, 184-191.

[11] Edward Schillebeeckx, *Christ the Sacrament of the Encounter with God* (Sheed & Ward: London, 1963) 54.

[12] All the symbols are identified in CCC #1234 to #1245. See also CCC #1147; CCC #1148; CCC #1155.

[13] CCC #1267.

[14] CCC#118.

[15] Schillebeeckx, Sacrament of Encounter, 77,79.

[16] Again, this is the theme of divine indwelling. Rahner, *Foundations*, 121-133.

[17] Again, this is the theme of divine indwelling. Rahner, *Foundations*, 121-133.

[18] Quote is From Cardinal Joseph Ratzinger, 'The Holy Spirit as Communio,' in *Communio* 25(Summer 1998); 324-327, 331.

[19] Peter Fransen SJ, *The New Life of Grace* (Geoffrey Chapman: London 1971) 52.

[20] CCC # 1265.

[21] Fransen *New life of Grace*, 81-98' Also Bausch, *A New Look at Sacraments*, 65-77.

[22] Fransen *New life of Grace*, 81-98. Also Bausch, *A New Look at Sacraments*, 65-77.

[23] Fransen, *New life*, 133.

[24] Bausch provides an introduction to the misunderstandings that collected around our practice of the sacraments in the opening chapters of his book *A New Look at Sacraments* (Mercier Press: Dublin, revised ed. 1983).

[25] CCC#1151.

[26] CCC # 1092.

[27] CCC #1088.

[28] CCC #1267 – 1269.

[29] His question is "What do you want from God's Church?"

[30] CCC #2002.

[31] See CCC # 2001.

[32] CCC #1235.

[33] Jeremiah 31:1.

[34] CCC # 197.

[35] . . .the love of God has been poured into our hearts by the Holy Spirit which has been given to us. Romans 5:5

[36] CCC # 1263.

[37] Anselm Grün OB expresses this fresh start beautifully when he says; 'By pouring water over a child we can see that he or she is not condemned to repeat the fates of his or her parents or grandparents, and is not merely a product of an ancestral line but can begin again in his or her own right.' Anselm Grün OB, *The Seven Sacraments*, trans. John Cumming (Continuum: London, 2003), 10.

[38] CCC #1265.

[39] See CCC #1997.

[40] CCC # 1266.

[41] CCC #1546; CCC # 1070.

[42] "Bausch, *New Look at Sacraments*, 17.

[43] Rahner, *Meditations on the Sacraments*, 5. CCC # 1997.

[44] Bausch, *New Look at Sacrament*, 21. See also CCC # 795.

[45] CCC #1257 CCC #1260 (GS 22 #5; LG 16; AG 7).

[46] Schillebeeckx, *Sacrament of Encounter* 77, 79.

CHAPTER SIX: THE NEARNESS OF YOU

[1] Andre Louf, *The Cistercian Way*, trans Nivard Kinsella, (Cistercian Publications, 1984) 73.

[2] Friedrich Von Hugel, *The Mystical element of Religion*, Volume 1 (J.M. Dent & Sons: London, 1923) 52-3.

[3] Breige O'Hare, 'Opening to Love; A Paradigm for Growth in relationship with God,' *Presence* (Spiritual Directors International) June, 2004, 27-36.

[4] Thomas Hart, *The Art of Christian Listening* (Paulist Press: New Jersey 1980) 79.

[5] Janet Ruffing, *Spiritual Direction: Beyond the Beginnings* (St Paul's: London, 2000) 125-9.

[6] Iain Matthew, *The Impact of God*, (Hodder and Stoughton: London 1995)78.

[7] Rahner, *Foundations*, 137.

[8] CCC #43; John of the Cross, 'Spiritual Canticle,' 1:3 in *The Collected Works of St John of the Cross*, trans Kieran Kavanaugh And Otilio Rodriguez (ICS Publications: Washington, 1991) 478.

[9] Further detail on this experience of darkness may be found in Thomas Green *When the Well Runs dry: Prayer Beyond the Beginnings* (Ave Maria Press: Notre Dame) 1998.

[10]O'Hare, 'Opening to Love,' 27-36.

[11] Spiritual Canticle 1:12 Kavanaugh and Rodriguez, *Collected Works of John of the Cross*, 478. See also: Ian Matthew, *The Impact of God*, 97.

[12] Abbot John Chapman, *Spiritual Letters* (Burns and Oates London, Reprint 2004). (First published 1935)

[13] Matthew, *Impact of God*, 90.

[14] John of the Cross, *Living Flame* 3: 46-7; this translation quoted in Iain Matthew, The Impact of God, 75.

[15] Laurence Jaffe, *Liberating the Heart: Spirituality and Jungian Psychology (Inner City Books: Toronto, 1990)* 84.

CHAPTER SEVEN: KNOWING WHAT MATTERS

[1] NT Wright, *Paul: Fresh Perspectives* (SPCK: London , 2005) 173. Not *Cognito ergo sum* (I think therefore I am) but *Amor, ergo sum* (I am loved, therefore I am) ref Romans 5:5-11, 8: 31-39.

[2] *Jerome* Vol 1; 29: 11.

[3] Karl Rahner SJ, *Meditations on the Sacraments* (Burn & Oates: London, 1977) 2-3.

[4] See: William A. Barry SJ and William J Connolly SJ, 'Criteria for evaluating religious experience,' in *The Practice of Spiritual direction (Harper Sanfrancisco No Date)* 101-117.

[5] Matthew, *The Impact of God, 51-58.*

[6] Wilkie Au & Noreen Connon, *Urgings of the Heart: A Spirituality of Integration (Paulist Press: New York, 1995)* 50; 133-156.

[7] *Jerome* Vol 2; 43: 118.

[8] *Jerome* Vol 2; 43: 119.

[9] *Jerome* Vol 2; 43: 119.

[10] This is thought to be a reference to the Feast of the three tabernacles, which commemorates the sojourn of the Israelites on Mount Sinai, when they received the Law through Moses. *Jerome* Vol 1; 43: 118

[11] Jerome Vol 2; 43: 118.

[12] Jerome Vol 2 43: 118.